TORAH TALK

AN EARLY CHILDHOOD TEACHING GUIDE

Yona Chubara · Miriam P. Feinberg · Rena Rotenberg

Alternatives in Religious Education, Inc.
Denver, Colorado

Published by:
Alternatives in Religious Education, Inc.
Denver, Colorado

Library of Congress Catalog Card Number 89-80336
ISBN Number 0-86705-023-3

Printed in the United States
10 9 8 7 6 5 4 3 2

CONTENTS

ACKNOWLEDGEMENTS

The completion of this work would not have been possible without the assistance, guidance, and enthusiasm of colleagues, friends, and most of all, family. The Jewish values which include love of Torah and of the Jewish people were imparted to us by Sylvia Polokoff and Nathan Polokoff (z"l), parents of Miriam Feinberg, and Mollie Rosenbaum and Herman Solomon Rosenbaum (z"l), parents of Rena Rosenberg. Their embodiment of many of the admirable values inherent in biblical personalities made the Bible stories more real to us.

The progress of our work was guided by the consistent encouragement of our husbands and children, Wolf, Saul, and Ester Tuby Rotenberg, Seth and Rachel Cutler Rotenberg, Ruth Gila Rotenberg, and the late Naomi Tova Rotenberg, and Mordecai, Jonathan, and Joshua Feinberg, and David and Deborah Feinberg Felsen. Their advice and patience created an atmosphere conducive to creativity.

We owe a debt of gratitude to teachers who enthusiastically field-tested our work and offered suggestions – Charlotte Muchnick, Ellen Neschis, Susan Bakhaj, Johanna Potts of Congregation Adas Israel in Washington, D.C.; Debbie Kaufman of
Congregation Tifereth Israel in Washington, D.C.; Sonny Herson, Sharon Wolfson, Eileen Weinstock, and Gale Pressman of Congregation Shaare Tefila in Silver Spring, Maryland; and Tema Sternberg, Netta Amir, and Susan Hefter of Congregation Ohr Kodesh in Chevy Chase, Maryland. Baltimore teachers who actively endorsed our work through creative classroom involvement are Elaine Blitzstein of Beth El Nursery and Kindergarten; Ellyn Soypher, Paula Berger, and Rachel Meisels of Chizuk Amuno Early Childhood Center; Toby Blake of the Solomon Schechter Day School; Saundra Madoff of Beth Israel Religious School; Cheryl Nanes of Beth Israel Kindergarten; Hattie Katkow of Bet Yeladim Nursery School; and Anita Needle of the Jewish Community Center/Owings Mills Nursery and Kindergarten.

We are grateful for opportunities to have consulted on the accuracy of our work with Mitchell Orlian, coordinator of the National Bible Contest of the World Zionist Organization's Department of Education and Culture and with Dr. Barry Gittlen, Professor of Biblical and Archaeological Studies at the Baltimore Hebrew University and Chairman of the Orlinsky Institute. We appreciate the encouragement and support of Dr. Emanuel Goldman and Rabbi Herbert Birnbaum, Executive Vice-President and Executive Director, respectively, of the Baltimore Board of Jewish Education, and of Miriam Snapir, Ofra Reisman, and Dvora Lifschitz of the World Zionist Organization. Nancy Nowak of Denver, Colorado was immensely helpful in suggesting expanded directions for the book.

To Kitty Wertheimer, Rebecca Isaacson, Kay Miller, Barbara Reiner, and

Marion Goldstein go our deepest thanks and appreciation for typing and retyping much of the work. Their assistance was invaluable.

Our very able editors, Rabbi Raymond A. Zwerin and Audrey Friedman Marcus of A.R.E. Publishing, recognized and improved upon the fruits of our labors in a most productive manner. We are extremely grateful to them.

FOREWORD

"The young child does not explore the world only in order to gain knowledge. All expressions of personality by the young child seem to be variations on one theme: the child's search for his life." (*The Personality of the Preschool Child: His Search for His Self* by Werner Wolff. New York: Grune & Stratton, 1946, p. 14)

The thrust of Early Childhood Education in recent years has been to concentrate on helping the child to understand his or her own experiences. While this approach has proven merit, in the process something else has usually been ignored. That something is an awareness of the value of traditional literature in enriching the intellectual and emotional life of the young child. Too often the curriculum of preschools has been limited to the here and now. Forgotten is the fact that the great stories of the past are great because they bespeak that which is timeless.

For Jewish Early Childhood Education, neglect of traditional materials is tragic. Such neglect deprives children of contact at an early age with our great literary treasures, and of the subsequent identification that would otherwise result. It also deprives them of the pleasure that comes from contact with stories of unique power and beauty. They miss the opportunity to develop early on the special kind of self-esteem that comes from knowing that one belongs to a people that has given the world some of its greatest spiritual gifts. Furthermore, the price of this early neglect is that for the first time in Jewish history, generations have grown up without the kind of basic Jewish literacy that was once common even among Jews of limited educational background. *Torah Talk: An Early Childhood Teaching Guide* is a thoughtful effort to bring the Hebrew Bible to the Jewish child.

It is well known that the Bible is an all time "best seller," having been published countless times and in innumerable languages. What is the key to its popularity, its power? The quest for meaning is probably innate. We need to understand ourselves and our world. We look to discover our strengths and to develop loving, supportive, dependable relationships with those around us. We also need to find and invest deeply in a cause that will give our lives moral significance.

The most famous of Jewish liturgical statements proclaims that God is One. It is this concept of the unity of the divine that enables us to envision a unity to the world and thus allows each of us to seek a sense of personal inner unity. Jewish images of God, particularly those found in the Bible, present God as a stable, integrated personality. (This is in stark contrast to images of divinity that abound in ancient pagan religious literature.) Because God is seen as being One (in all the meanings of that word), acting out of a set of certain values, so, too, our personal integration follows from knowing and accepting those same values, incorporating them into our daily behavior, and making them the basis of our major life-commitments.

In Torah we find such Jewish values as *tzedakah, hachnassat orechim, tzedek, chesed, emet, kedushah,* etc. In its stories we are also presented with accounts of and models of human beings who struggle to maintain those values in the face of real challenges posed by activity in the world. The people we meet in the Bible faced the same problems we face today in our lives. The relationships therein between parent and child, siblings, husband and wife, friends, neighbors, strangers, the rich and the poor, the mighty and the humble, are a mirror of our relationships today.

Moreover, Jewish tradition encourages people to read the text actively and to create their own interpretations. Some of these interpretations have become widely known; others remain personal. Such "Midrash making" is both enjoyable and profoundly important because it provides a screen upon which we can project our problems, our hopes, our relationships. In addition, the collections of biblical commentaries and Midrashim are among the best sources of information about the world of those who wrote them. They are internal history at its best, the record of how people reacted to the issues that engaged their minds and hearts.

Yet, without access to these stories written in a language understandable to children, the text is as good as closed to the very young. That is the beauty of *Torah Talk*. For parents, this book opens the opportunity to renew or enrich interaction with children at home. Two times suggest themselves in particular. One is mealtime, especially Shabbat and *Yom Tov* meals, when reading and discussing the stories can provide wonderful subject matter for meaningful discussion. The other is the bedtime hour when the reading of (some of) these stories can trigger a discussion that engages the child's mind. If such a discussion ends with the recitation of the *Shema* (which implies God's protective care for children) it can become the kind of ritual which allows the day to end restfully and strengthens the sense of a child's well-being. Jewish education is the process of creating memories and, will it or not, the parent is destined to be the prime educator of his or her child.

Some parents or teachers avoid using the Bible as a prime resource because they think that some of the stories are inappropriate for young children. The work of Bruno Bettelheim, among others, has shown us that young children thrive emotionally and intellectually on rich literary fare. Of course, not every Bible story is appropriate for young children. The authors of this book have carefully chosen those biblical accounts that can build self-esteem while stimulating a child's mind as well. Yet, they have not shied away from the kind of conflict that is real to the child and therefore apt to engage his or her attention. Moreover, stories learned through this book are true to the spirit of the original text. There is no material here that will have to be unlearned at a later age.

Some parents or teachers have avoided using Bible stories because of a lack of confidence in their ability to teach material that raises, for them, unresolved religious questions. With all respect for the sincerity of those concerns, they are, to my mind, misplaced. The Bible itself raises virtually every religious question that has been asked. It also offers more than one answer to the questions. It is part of the glory of Judaism that it encourages intellectual honesty and creative thought in dealing with matters of faith and theology. Besides the Bible, the entire corpus of Rabbinic literature is replete with examples of individuals who challenged God when life was painful, alongside examples of God's fulfillment of the Covenant. "The Seal of the Holy One, Blessed be He, is Truth" (*Babylonian Talmud*).

The child can only be enriched by the feeling that the issues raised in the Bible are not "childish," but instead are important enough to engage the thinking of valued adults. Thus, there is nothing wrong with a teacher sharing the sense of wonder and perplexity at the behavior of biblical characters. "I don't know," or "You've given me something to think about," or "Sometimes I wonder about that myself," are respectable and acceptable responses on the part of parent and teacher.

Finally, in the matter of self-esteem, it is enriching to any human being (particularly one who is young) to feel a part of that which is lasting and valuable. Jewish peoplehood provides the child with a ready sense of lineage, of roots in a tradition that combines the universal and the particular dimensions of culture and religion in a way that has been most remarkable. Introducing the child and the family to the Bible, the greatest of Jewish creations, is a way of telling that child, "You are a part of a family whose earliest memories go back to the dawn of religious tradition. You share that lineage with millions of other children and adults around the world. You are a Jew and your people has given the world its greatest book." Even the youngest child can feel good about being part of such a heritage. That child deserves to feel good; the covenant is part of his/her birthright, and to learn and identify with its stories are part of his/her task and privilege.

In summary, Bible study at home and in the preschool provides exposure for child and adult to important issues presented in an exciting and compelling fashion. It allows the child and the adult to exchange ideas and feelings about the relationships of human beings. It challenges each to think about what it means to be a person and a Jew. It instills a sense of pride in the contributions of the tradition shared by adult and child. It offers opportunities to learn, preserve, and enrich that tradition. Investment of time and energy will yield great benefit to adult and child now and, hopefully, will lead to a lifelong love affair with the Bible.

Saul P. Wachs
Chair of the Department of Education
Gratz College, Philadelphia
Nisan, 5749

INTRODUCTION

The Beginnings

This book has its origin in a chance event. Miriam Snapir, formerly Early Childhood Consultant for the World Zionist Organization in North America, learned of a creative new project initiated by her successor, Yona Chubara. Yona had begun work on stories and activities designed to teach Bible to young children.

Miriam felt that such a book would be an important contribution to the field of early childhood education. In her interactions with educators throughout North America, she had observed a hesitancy to teach Bible to young children. Many teachers avoided the subject because they were unfamiliar with the stories or uncomfortable dealing with the Bible. Others complained that renditions of Bible stories available were not appropriate for the age level. Looking into this common complaint, Miriam did indeed discover a paucity of commercially produced Bible materials which were, at the same time, developmentally appropriate and true to the original text.

At approximately the same time, Ofra Reisman, Director of the Department of Early Childhood Education of the David Yellin Teachers College in Jerusalem, presented a series of workshops to early childhood teachers throughout the United States on teaching Bible to young children. The enthusiastic response of the participants in those workshops further indicated the need for teaching Bible to young children, as well as for the materials for doing so. Her ideas greatly influenced the development of this book.

At Miriam Snapir's suggestion, Miriam P. Feinberg, Early Childhood Consultant with the Board of Jewish Education of Greater Washington, D.C., and Rena Rotenberg, Early Childhood Consultant with the Board of Jewish Education of Baltimore, began their collaboration, developing Yona Chubara's preliminary efforts into the stories and activities which comprise this work.

As *Torah Talk: An Early Childhood Teaching Guide* took shape, it was field-tested in Jewish nurseries, kindergartens, and supplementary schools in Baltimore and Washington, D.C. Many of the ideas recommended by teachers involved in the field-testing were incorporated.

Are Bible Stories Appropriate for Young Children

Teaching Bible to children of preschool and kindergarten age raises many questions among parents and teachers: Will children this young be able to understand the historical placement of the stories? Are the stories meaningless because their geographic placement is so remote? Are the values in Bible stories contradictory and/or confusing to children this age? Will such stories need to be unlearned and then relearned in different versions at later ages? Is the language of the stories appropriate, and can children comprehend the complicated meanings and nuances in the text? Is the presentation of angels or of God conceptually confusing? Are the mores of biblical times so different from ours as to make their presentation too difficult? Are name changes too hard for children to grasp? Before preceding further, let us address each of these questions.

Historical Placement

While it is true that young children are unable to place the biblical events in their proper historical context, this is no reason to avoid teaching Bible stories. Historical placement is of little significance when introducing any information to young children. They may not understand the concept of "three thousand years ago," but their understanding of a sequence of events has certainly begun to develop. For this reason, the stories here are presented in a chronological sequence, starting with Abraham, followed by Isaac, and then by Jacob, etc.

Geographical Placement

It is of little importance for young children to know the precise locale of stories which are read to them. Children of this age are already accustomed to hearing tales which take place not only "once upon a time," but also in exotic, faraway places. We read these tales even though preschool children cannot place the stories geographically. Therefore, whether Haran or Egypt or the land of Israel is as close as the neighborhood supermarket or as far away as the land of Oz is immaterial.

Introduction of Biblical Values

Early childhood is a critical period. It is at this time that the development of moral concepts begins. Values and attitudes are often internalized without being processed and without being fully understood, to be manifested only at a later age. Bible stories poignantly introduce Jewish and universally accepted human values. When taught properly, these stories can enrich a child's identity as a Jew and can provide a solid and positive moral foundation.

There are those who would hold off introducing the Bible until children are beyond the early childhood years. Such an arbitrary opinion could just as well lead to a position of not telling any stories to children until they are ready to understand them in all of their ramifications. Therefore, why discriminate especially against biblical accounts which are at the heart and soul of our people's history? Perhaps the concern of those who would delay the introduction of Bible stories is really with those biblical accounts which would clearly perplex or frighten the young students (e.g, the binding of Isaac, Judah and Tamar, sending Hagar away, etc.). Without a doubt, those passages are better presented to an older age group, to students who have developed the necessary maturity to integrate these far more complex concepts.

But the Bible stories included in this book certainly may, indeed should, be told to the very young, because they are among the best literature to read and teach to our earliest learners. The stories are logical and pleasing, rather than confusing or frightening. The values exemplified are based on human concerns and interpersonal relations which are very much within the ken of the very young child. Deleted from the stories is information inappropriate for the age group, and omitted altogether are those stories which raise questions or contain moral dilemmas with which the child cannot cope.

An early introduction to Bible will foster in children a comfort with the biblical milieu and will help them to form roots with their past. Children can begin to internalize the values exemplified in the family stories of Abraham and of Jacob and their progeny. They can begin to wrestle with the conflicts that beset our ancestors and see how those problems were resolved. As our children mature, they will learn these stories in still greater depth, developing a far richer appreciation for, and identification with, these early leaders and events.

Building on the Stories

If, as in this book, the Bible stories remain faithful to the original text, it will not be necessary for children to unlearn anything at a later time. Instead, as the child matures, the stories need merely be fleshed out and other stories added. The stories are like earliest paint on good canvas – nothing need be removed for the next layer to be applied. That which came first serves as a solid base for all that follows. In many other anthologies of Bible stories, Midrash and Bible are presented together. In such cases the young child is not capable of distinguishing the original text from the Midrashic legend, and this leads to confusion. Therefore, in this book, no Midrashic material has been added to the stories.

The Biblical Language

It is certainly true that the unabridged language of the actual Bible text is too difficult and, therefore, inappropriate for young children. It is also true that the text is filled with layers of meaning and complex nuances. Because of these difficulties, the stories in *Torah Talk* have all been rewritten in language which can be easily understood by young children.

The literary style of the Bible is terse, and descriptive passages are few and far between. The only liberties taken in retelling these stories for the very young lies in the minimal fleshing out of conversations and adapting dialogue, as needed, to match the vocabulary to the age group and to bring the action closer to a child's frame of reference. When appropriate, historical and archaeological information, (e.g., dwellings, occupations, modes of transportation, climate, topography, native animals, and household furnishings) has been included. As stated before, however, the stories have remained faithful to the text throughout.

Angels and God

It has been posited that ghosts and angels are a part of the collective unconscious. Cartoons on television have certainly exploited the fascination that children have with them. While most children have been exposed to many hours of such cartoons by the time they reach preschool, it is also quite possible that the concept of angels may be too confusing conceptually for young children. Therefore, when the Torah text refers to angels, the action which follows is recorded in the telling of the stories, but the angels are not identified as such (e.g., the three who visit Abraham are correctly referred to as "guests").

In Genesis 32:25-30, Jacob wrestles with an angel who appears in the form of a man. This account is not included in this book. While this encounter is a significant event in Jacob's life, it involves ideas and images which are too complex and confusing for children of this age. Nevertheless, the account of Jacob's move from Laban's home to Canaan was not eliminated because it provides an important link between two elements of Jacob's life – the establishment of his family and the settling of his family in the land of Canaan.

In the Torah, God operates (*kevayachol*) in different modes – as the Creator; the omnipotent, omniscient, and omnipresent Ruler; the compassionate Father; the just Ruler; the jealous and angry Ruler who brings retribution for the sins of the people, etc. Admittedly, this seeming multiplicity of roles could also be conceptually confusing for young children. Therefore, the stories in this book avoid theological and philosophical references to or interpretations of God. God's active involvement with the Hebrew people is handled when it occurs in the text in a simple and straightforward manner, and conversations between God and the Hebrews are reported in ways that will stimulate candid discussions in the classroom.

Different Mores

The mores of the people of Israel frequently differ from those of our society and this can be problematic for young children. For instance, the existence of multiple wives and concubines for the patriarchs is particularly challenging to explain. Yet, how do we tell the story of Jacob without telling about both Leah and Rachel? Simply put, it is not possible to be faithful to the text while avoiding all such difficulties. The principle employed here is that when such elements are necessary to the story, they are presented in a very direct fashion. For example, concerning Jacob's wives who are essential to the continuity of the story, children can be told that it was an accepted standard of behavior in biblical times to have more than one wife and that this differs from our standard today. On the other hand, because they are not critical to the continuity of the story, Hagar, Zilpah, and Bilhah have not been included.

Name Changes

It is doubtful that the changing of a name in a biblical personality would be terribly problematic for young children or difficult for a child to grasp. After all, children today have a first and last and usually a middle name. Most Jewish children know that they also have a Hebrew or Yiddish name, as do their Jewish parents. Hyphenated family names are commonplace, as are pet names. Most children are called by the affectionate or diminutive form of their real name – Robert is called Bobby or Bud, Shoshanah is called Shoshi or Suzie, etc. – and children seem to understand that changing a name is a part of life. They especially understand that when a parent is angry, he or she is most likely to call the child by the full and formal name, but when all is going smoothly, the affectionate form of the child's name is most likely to be used. In these stories, for the sake of simplicity, some of these name changes are not mentioned (such as Abram to Abraham and Sarai to Sarah). However, the name changes of both Jacob and Joseph are mentioned, as they are events crucial to the story's continuity.

Summary

The above considerations make it clear that not only are selected Bible stories suitable for telling to young children, but it is especially appropriate and important that we tell them. In summary, this is why these stories are age appropriate:

1. The plots are simple, involving only a few central characters, thus enabling the child to follow the story with ease and to identify with it.
2. Biblical descriptions are short and specific, thereby holding the attention of the young listener.
3. Emotions are generally expressed by action (i.e., love by an embrace, grief by weeping, rage by shouting, etc.). Young children can understand such specific illustrations of emotions.
4. Biblical images are concrete because the language of the Bible includes few adjectives and many verbs. This helps to engage the mental and imaginative powers of youngsters.
5. Biblical characters are human rather than idealized. Their good and bad deeds are presented in a balanced manner, making them believable to the child.

About This Book

The purpose of this book is to help a teacher or parent to introduce the young learner, ages 3 to 6, to the events depicted in the first five books of the Bible – his or her biblical heritage. There are nineteen chapters in this book, each containing from one to five short biblical narratives. The first chapter introduces Abraham just as he is told by God to leave his birthplace and to go to Canaan with Sarah and their household. The child learns about the travels of Abraham and Sarah to their new home, their desire to establish a family there, and God's promise to help them do so. Subsequent stories follow in chronological order, establishing a sense of the family line from Abraham to Isaac to Jacob to Joseph, and then to Moses. The last narrative is about the children of Israel at Mt. Sinai. Each chapter contains the following sections:

Table of Contents
A Table of Contents is placed at the beginning of each chapter to serve as a handy guide for finding page numbers for each section of that chapter. It is a ready reference to the elements of the story and to the major themes that are about to be shared with the children.

Before Telling the Stories

This section is as useful as it is unusual. Learning, much like any physical activity, benefits from a preliminary "warm up," so to speak. It is important that the listener come to the story in the right frame of reference. Terminology should be understood before it is confronted in the story; the stage for what is about to be heard should be set. This section is intended to do all of the above – establishing continuity with events past and setting the tone for events to come.

Telling the Story

This section contains the biblical story itself, adapted for the early childhood level. All of the stories are set in larger type so that they may be read more easily. Each story has been divided into short segments geared to the attention span of the audience. Therefore, the sharing of these stories with the children should prove to be a comfortable, easy experience for the reader. Following each segment are questions to discuss with the children. These questions are based strictly on information in the story. They are best used as but a brief interval between the reading of story segments in the chapter.

Themes in the Story

Here you will find an outline of themes present in the story just told, as well as discussion questions for each theme under the heading "Bringing the Theme Closer." The inclusion of the themes will give a focus for the teacher or parent when discussing the story with the children. The questions in this section are intended to bring the story closer to the personal day-to-day life of the young listener.

Creative Follow-up

In every chapter there are many follow-up activities. These include a wide variety of exercises which are categorized under such headings as: Retelling the Story, Role Play, Music, Building/Creating, Game Time, Experience Chart, etc. Each of these activities is designated for three and four-year-olds, for five and six-year-olds, or for three to six-year-olds. Under each you will find goals (either for both similar activities or for each activity under a specific age group, a description of the activity, the materials needed, and the procedure to follow.)

Taking the Story Home

At the conclusion of the Creative Follow-up is a home component section which includes activities on the story for parents and children. It is recommended that the teacher send home a letter at the beginning of the year outlining the curriculum and informing parents of the home component which accompanies the stories. Then, as often as possible, send home a synopsis of a story, along with a listing of suggested activities for parent or parents to do with their child.

Teaching Recommendations

When To Tell Bible Stories

It is a good idea to begin telling the stories immediately after Simchat Torah so that you can connect the Bible to this holiday. Whenever possible, in fact, connect the telling of the other stories with corresponding holidays, such as the story of the Exodus from Egypt, which can be told before Passover. It is preferable to select a particular time during the week (once or twice a week) for telling Bible stories. Friday, within the framework of "welcoming the Sabbath," or Monday and Thursday (days when the Torah is read in the synagogue), are recommended in a five day school. Ideally, children will recognize the storytelling hour as a special time and will look forward to it.

How To Tell the Stories

The main objective is to tell a story in such a way that children can follow what is happening and respond appropriately. Before you begin to tell a story, take the time to prepare the children for what will follow. Create a special environment. Involve the children by reviewing highlights of the previous story. They can fill in pertinent details of the story told previously, thus guaranteeing continuity. It is helpful to sit in the same place for each storytelling session and to do a specific song or finger play in order to create a particular mood. Tell the story in a sprightly manner that will make the words come alive, encouraging the children to imagine the events and the atmosphere of the story. Try not to dwell on information that is outside of the story, so as not to break the continuity of the story.

Keep the discussions short after each segment of the story. It is intentional that the discussion questions which follow each segment are short and that they require short answers. These questions help the children to understand what has already happened in a way that does not interrupt the sequence of the story or allow the attention of the children to stray.

It is well known that young children learn by doing. The more opportunities for reinforcing the ideas that are presented through concrete experiences, the more the child is capable of internalizing the new information. The more varied the concrete experiences, the greater are the opportunities for reaching all of the children. Therefore, involve students in as many as possible of the creative follow-up activities outlined herein.

Reinforcement Opportunities

You will find frequent mention throughout this book of opening circle, free choice activities, final circle, and pre-Shabbat party. These terms are clarified below. All of these occasions provide an opportunity to integrate Bible stories into other segments of the daily schedule. When introduced at these additional times, the material in this book is reinforced and further internalized. Finally, reference is often made to the use of experience charts and illustrations. These are also described below.

Opening Circle

Opening circle helps the children and teacher to begin the school day. During this time, all of the children sit together in a circle on the floor (or on chairs if preferred). In the fortunate situation that there are two competent and trained adults in the classroom, the group can be divided in half and each adult can lead a small circle. (Arrange the two circles as far as possible from each other.)

Teachers generally use circle time for taking attendance, providing the children with the opportunity to share experiences with each other, and informing the children of the plans for the day. Other suggestions for using circle time to good advantage are: saying daily prayers; teaching (or reviewing) a song; joining in a fingerplay or reciting a poem; and discussing the calendar, the weather, and the free choice activity centers in the classroom. This time can also be used to review biblical material and/or to inform children about the new Bible story to be introduced during class that day.

Free Choice Activities

Some experienced teachers may feel comfortable providing as many as eight activity centers simultaneously. However, most teachers offer fewer than eight, and four is an acceptable number. The centers can be changed so that in the period of a month, many choices have been offered. Encourage children to use the activity centers to develop creative play while interacting with their peers.

The centers generally offered on a regular basis are housekeeping, block building, art, and table toys/manipulatives. Other centers which should be offered, at least periodically, are: sand, water, music and movement, library, large-muscle area, woodworking, and science.

A Jewish classroom should also provide a Judaic center in which Shabbat and Jewish holiday objects and pictures can be displayed on a regular basis. In addition, the introduction of a Bible center is an effective way to reinforce the Bible stories which were introduced during story time. This center can include photographs of the terrain and vegetation in Israel; pictures of tents, wells, and biblical animals; puppets relating to Bible stories; and children's drawings.

Final Circle

Many teachers find it useful to bring children together for a final circle at the end of the school day. Once again, this can be accomplished by arranging the children either in a single large circle or in two small circles. Some teachers prefer to read a story at this time; others use the time for reviewing the events of the day in a relaxed, happy manner. In the latter instance, all of the children should be given an opportunity to speak during the final circle time. Encourage the children to talk about the biblical stories and the Creative Follow-up activities in which they participated.

Pre-Shabbat Party

The pre-Shabbat party is an essential time to emphasize the regularity and specialness of Shabbat. The children need to be aware, however, that the party does not signify the beginning of Shabbat, but that it is a preparation for Shabbat which will occur that evening (if the party is on Friday) or the next evening (if the party is on Thursday). The pre-Shabbat party is an appropriate time to tell a Bible story, emphasizing the connection between Torah reading and Shabbat.

To ensure consistency and to set the mood, always have a real Bible in your hand. Refer to the Torah scroll that is in the *Aron Kodesh* in the synagogue as the source of all of our information and knowledge about biblical personalities and events. Always tell the children that each week on Shabbat another portion of the Torah is read in the synagogue, and that at that time, one person reads from the Torah scroll and the others follow along in a Bible or listen carefully.

On occasion, take the children to a synagogue. Before the open Ark, tell a Bible story. While it may not always be possible to do all the creative follow-up activities at this site, it is always possible – and desirable – to lead a discussion there with the children about the story read. Introduce the other activities during the ensuing days, thus demonstrating that Bible activities are ongoing.

Experience Charts

As a follow-up to the Bible stories, the use of experience charts is an effective way to find out what the children have learned. They also provide an opportunity for children to teach each other by sharing information. An experience chart should be viewed as an extension of a classroom discussion. A description of how to make and use experience charts follows.

Materials

large pieces of newsprint (lined or unlined)
an easel on which to attach the newsprint (or masking tape with which
    to attach the newsprint to a wall or chalkboard)
dark felt marker or crayon

Procedure

1. Following a discussion, ask the children to provide additional ideas on the topic discussed.
2. Write those ideas (use sentences or single words) on the paper. If the children are too young to read, use pictures instead of, or in addition to, words. The experience chart should be no longer than a single page. The print should be clear, large, dark, and consistent, starting at the top and proceeding to the bottom of the page.
3. When the exercise is completed, review the chart with the children, asking them to "read" its contents. Two examples of experience charts follow:

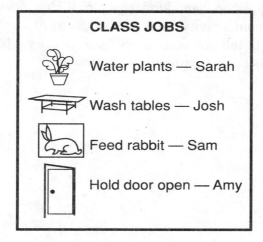

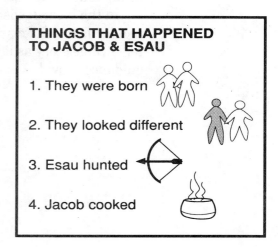

Illustrations

A carefully considered decision has been made to exclude illustrations of specific Bible characters. The use of such illustrations should be delayed until the children themselves have developed a mental image of the lives of the Bible people and their life styles. Once children have shared their personal impressions through a variety of creative media, they can be exposed to artists' renditions. In the meantime, the children may be introduced to pictures showing the land of Israel, its vegetation and animal life, as well as a variety of tents and wells which are common in the Middle East, and generic biblical and Egyptian people. Illustrations of this nature may be found at the back of this book. You will find many uses for these pictures. For example, you may show them to the children at appropriate times when you are telling the stories, you might use them for bulletin boards, and you may wish to make copies of them for the children to color.

Conclusion

The inclusion on a regular basis of appropriate Bible stories will enable children to become familiar with the concept of the people of Israel, to identify with the central biblical events, and to learn about and identify with the lives and interactions of biblical heroes and heroines. Through age appropriate discussions and follow-up activities, this introduction to the Bible can be a very positive experience, providing background and tools for understanding the Bible on an adult level and resulting in lifelong identification with our ancestors.

In the ideal Jewish preschool and kindergarten, Bible stories should be a regular feature of classroom activity. It should be just as natural for a teacher to tell a Bible story as it is to tell any other story appropriate to children. With the guidance provided in this book, that ideal can be realized.

CHAPTER 1

Abraham

BEFORE TELLING THE STORY

1. Discuss with the children people they know who are very important to them. Have them explain why each of these people is important.

2. Introduce the idea that a person named Abraham lived a long, long time ago. Stress the fact that even though we did not know him as a living person, we know some things about him that are very important to the Jewish people today. Present an experience chart to the children headed "Things We Know About Abraham." Encourage the children to dictate ideas for the chart and write the ideas down.

   Now present a second experience chart with the heading, "Things We Wish We Knew About Abraham." Encourage children to suggest ideas to add to this experience chart (e.g., what Abraham looked like, etc.), and write the ideas down.

3. Introduce the children to the Bible.

   a. Show a Bible in Hebrew and English. Point out the Hebrew lettering and encourage the children to note differences between the Hebrew and the English. Draw the children's attention to the fact that there are no pictures in the Bible.

   b. While holding the text on your lap, tell the story of Abraham. Let the children know that although you are telling the story in English, the original story was written in Hebrew.

   c. Show the children a Torah scroll. Point out the Hebrew script and discuss the absence of the English translation and of pictures. Find the story of Abraham in the Torah and let the children see it. Invite a Rabbi or other individual to retell the story by reading parts of it from the actual Torah.

   d. Note the differences between the Torah scroll and the printed Bible. Compare both of these to illustrated storybooks with which the children are familiar.

   e. Discuss the importance of the Torah to the Jewish people. Talk about the ways in which we demonstrate our respect for the Torah (e.g., we keep it in a special place in the synagogue; we dress it in a special cover and decorate it with beautiful ornaments; we bring it out to read on every Shabbat, on Mondays, on Thursdays, and on holidays; we carry it carefully around during a worship service so that we can kiss it, etc.).

TELLING THE STORY

Abraham and Sarah

Many years ago Abraham and his wife Sarah lived in a tent. Abraham was a shepherd. He took care of sheep. Every morning he would take the sheep to a field to graze.

One day when Abraham was in the field with his sheep, he started thinking.

"I'll sit down here for a while," he said to himself. "The sky is so clear and blue today. The bird in that tree over there is so beautiful. Everything around me is beautiful, and I am a lucky man! Sarah is a good wife! She takes good care of me."

Meanwhile, back home in the tent, Sarah was cooking. She thought, "Abraham will be coming back soon. He'll be tired and hot and hungry. I'll make those cakes that he likes so much and he'll have some cold milk. That's always good to drink on a hot day." As she got everything ready, she thought, "I am a lucky woman. Abraham is a good husband. He takes good care of me."

Abraham sat in the field thinking. He looked around him. He looked at the sheep. He looked at the water and at the trees and at the grass and at the clouds in the sky. He wondered as he looked. "Who made all this?" he thought. "Somebody made it."

Suddenly Abraham heard a voice talking to him.

"Abraham, leave your country. Leave your father's house and go to another country which I will show you. You and Sarah must go to live in Canaan. I am God and I am telling you what to do." At first Abraham didn't know what to say. He was confused. Then God said, "I will take care of you and your children there and you will pray to Me."

Abraham said, "But Sarah and I don't have any children."

"You will have children," said God.

Abraham was surprised and excited! He thought, "I must listen to God. Now I need to hurry back to tell Sarah what just happened!"

Questions on the Story

1. Why do you think Abraham has agreed to leave his home and go to a strange country?
2. Why was Abraham excited to leave his home and move to Canaan? Was Abraham a little confused too?

Leaving Haran

The sun was beginning to set as Abraham came home. He heard Sarah singing.

Sarah came out of the tent. "Abraham you're home," she said. "I heard the sheep baa-ing. You must be tired. Come in and rest."

She looked at Abraham's face. She could tell that something important had happened.

"Sarah, listen," said Abraham, "something very unusual has happened! Today while I was in the field with the sheep, I noticed that everything seemed more beautiful than ever. Suddenly I heard a voice. It was God talking to me, telling me to leave the country where we live, and to go to another country which God will show me. Can you imagine that? God wants us to move to a different land."

"But where? How will we get there? We won't know anyone there," said Sarah.

"Don't worry, Sarah," said Abraham. "My nephew Lot will go with us. We'll have food and a good home. Most important of all, God will help us, and God has promised that we'll have children. Isn't that thrilling?"

Sarah was caught up in Abraham's excitement. She thought, "We must all help to get ready for the trip. Abraham will pack the tent. Lot will get the animals ready, and I will prepare the food. If Abraham wants to go, I'll go with him."

Questions on the Story

1. How did Sarah know that something important had happened to Abraham while he was tending the sheep?

2. What did Sarah say about Abraham's important news?
3. What did Abraham and Sarah take with them for the trip and for their new home in the new country? (Make sure that the children mention the animals, their workers, food, clothes, etc.)

A Long Journey

Everyone was busy getting ready for the trip to the land of Canaan. Sarah felt sad to be leaving Haran. She and Abraham had lived there for a long time.

Abraham could see that Sarah was sad. "Don't worry, Sarah," he said. "With God's help we'll have a good home and we'll have children in the land of Canaan." Sarah smiled as she thought about their new home.

Abraham and Sarah and Lot were ready to leave. They kissed and hugged and said good-bye to their family. Then they started on their trip to Canaan with their servants and their animals.

"Baa, baa" called the sheep.

"Klop, klop" went the feet of the donkeys.

"Jingle, jingle" rang the small bells on the goats.

The sheep walked together. The donkeys moved slowly, taking big steps and carrying big sacks.

Sarah sat on one of the donkeys. Abraham walked nearby. Lot watched the animals so that they would not get lost. They all walked and walked and walked toward Canaan until it began to get dark.

"Let's stop here and rest for the night," said Abraham, and he began to set up his tent.

"I'll get some food ready so that we can eat together," said Sarah. Then she took some flour from a sack and began to make bread.

The next day they started out again. Sarah, Abraham, and Lot and all their sheep and cattle and servants walked together toward Canaan. They walked that whole day. Then they walked the next day. They kept walking day after day, but they always stopped to eat and to rest for the night.

At last, one day, they reached Canaan. They felt tired, but very happy. They looked around until they found a good place to live.

"This looks like a good place for us," said Abraham. It was near a big field. The tired travelers set up tents. "Thank you, God, for helping us to get here," they all said. They were happy that their trip had ended.

Questions on the Story

1. Why do you think Sarah smiled when she thought about her new home?
2. Why do you think Sarah and Abraham had to take so many animals, sacks of food, and tents with them?
3. How did Sarah and Abraham and Lot feel when they finally reached Canaan? What did they do when they arrived?

A New Home

Abraham, Sarah, and Lot lived in the land of Canaan. Many years passed. They became older. Their hair turned grey, and there were some wrinkles on their faces.

One day Sarah said, "Abraham, a long time ago before we left Haran, you told me something very important. You said that God promised that we would have children here in the land of Canaan. But now we are old and we still don't have any children."

Abraham sat quietly. He thought, "God did tell me that Sarah and I would have children, but it hasn't happened." As he thought about it, he became sad.

Abraham went out for a walk. He walked slowly and quietly. He was thinking. He thought about what it would be like to have a child. He thought how nice it would be to play and sing and talk with the child, to teach the child how to take care of the sheep and cattle, to talk to the child about the land of Canaan and about God.

Suddenly Abraham heard a sound. God was talking to him. "Don't worry, Abraham, you and Sarah will have a son, and your son will have children. Look up at the sky. Can you count the stars? That's how many children and grandchildren your children will have."

Abraham was so surprised that he didn't know what to do first.

"I must go right away to tell Sarah the good news!" he shouted. He didn't walk, he ran, as fast as his legs would carry him.

At last he was back with Sarah. He could see that she had been crying. He sat down next to her. He smiled a big, happy smile and hugged her.

"Sarah, don't worry," he said. "We will have a child. God will help us. God helped us to go from Haran to Canaan and God will help us again! You'll see!"

Sarah looked at Abraham's happy face. She thought, "Maybe he's right."

Questions on the Story

1. Was it important to Abraham and Sarah to have a baby? How do you know that?
2. Can you count the stars in the sky? How many do you think there are? Do you think Abraham will have a big family or a small one?
3. Abraham and Sarah mentioned many times in the story that they didn't have a child. Why do you think they mentioned it so often? (5 and 6-year olds)

THEMES IN THE STORY

Abraham Leaves His Home

Leaving home and moving to an unknown country is a difficult undertaking. Abraham was willing to make such a move because he had faith in God.

Bringing the Theme Closer

- What do you think Abraham and Sarah said to their family and friends before they left for their new home?

- Did you ever move to a new home? How did you prepare for moving? (Encourage the children who have experienced this to share the information with others.)
- What did you take with you from your old home? What is it like to move to a new house or apartment?
- What did you say to your old friends and neighbors when you left?
- Why did you move to a new place? Do you like it? Do you want to move to a new place again? Why?
- Do you think Abraham could have found out anything about his new home before he went there? (5 and 6-year-olds)
- What would you have done if you were Abraham or Sarah? (5 and 6-year-olds)

Abraham and Sarah Want To Have Children

Abraham and Sarah wish for a baby and are very sad that they do not have a child.

Bringing the Theme Closer
- Help children to relate to the problem of Abraham and Sarah so that they will understand the idea that it is a Jewish value for children to be a part of a family and the idea of handing things down from generation to generation.

God's Promise and Abraham's Faith in God

Abraham was a man of faith, a true believer in God. Although he questioned God's intentions at times, he always acquiesced when God directed him to do a particular task.

Bringing the Theme Closer
- Discuss God's promise to Abraham. Was God's promise good? Why? Why do you think God gave the promise to Abraham? What do you think God thought about Abraham? How do you know that? Does Abraham believe that he and Sarah will have a baby as God promised him? How do you know?

CREATIVE FOLLOW UP

Retelling the Story

Goals

To reinforce information acquired during the telling of the story.
To help the children sequence the events of the story.

HAND PUPPETS (3 AND 4-YEAR-OLDS)

Description of Activity

Children use puppets to talk about characters in the story.

Materials

an assortment of hand puppets

(Note: It is not necessary to provide puppets that look like the people or animals in the story. When the children are provided with nondescript materials, they can impose their own ideas on them and change their ideas at will.)

Procedure

1. Form a group of 3 or 4 children while the others are involved in free choice activities.
2. Give each child in the group a puppet that represents one character in the story.
3. The teacher acts as narrator and begins to tell the story. Each child holds up his/her puppet and speaks the part of the assigned character.
4. Continue in this manner for no longer than ten minutes.
5. Repeat this procedure with other children, a few at a time, until all those who wish to participate have done so. Use the puppets to tell the story again at a pre-Shabbat party.

HAND PUPPETS (5 AND 6-YEAR-OLDS)

Description of Activity

Children tell their own version of the story using puppets.

Materials

2 hand puppets of any kind

Procedure

1. Following the initial storytelling, the teacher holds up puppets representing Abraham and Sarah and begins to retell the story.
2. After telling a part of the story, the teacher passes the puppets to a child who continues to tell the story while manipulating the puppets.
3. When the teacher holds up his/her hand, the child passes the puppets to another child who continues in the same manner.
4. This procedure continues until the entire story has been told or, if there is time, until each of the children has taken a turn.
5. If everyone has not had a turn, repeat this activity on subsequent occasions.

Building/Creating

Goals

To find out how much the children remember about the story.
To encourage the internalizing of the story.

COLLAGE (3 AND 4-YEAR-OLDS)

Description of Activity

Children review the story by creating collages.

Materials

fabric
glue
scissors
yarn
pipe cleaners
cotton balls
construction paper

Procedure

1. Review the story with the children.
2. Arrange for all materials to be easily accessible. Invite children to use the materials in small groups during the free play time. If necessary,

extend this activity over 2 or 3 days in order to provide an opportunity for each of the children to participate in a small group.

3. After they have completed their pictures, the children may show and describe them to the rest of the class.

PLAY DOUGH (5 AND 6-YEAR-OLDS)

Description of Activity

Out of play dough children create the shapes of animals which might have traveled to Canaan with Abraham.

Materials

pictures of sheep, goats, camels
play dough (store bought or made with the following recipe)

Procedure

1. Share pictures of sheep, goats, and camels to initiate a discussion of animals which existed in Bible times.
2. Encourage children to describe the animals, as well as the kinds of food they ate. Discuss whether or not the animals were able to carry provisions for the trip.
3. Invite the children to participate in making play dough according to the recipe below (or use the ready-made variety).
4. Invite the children to manipulate the play dough and to use it to make the shapes of animals which they think existed in Abraham's time.
5. Have children show and describe their animals to their classmates.
6. Place the animals in the Bible corner so that the children can continue to enjoy seeing them.

Play Dough

Ingredients

4 cups flour
$\frac{1}{4}$ cup salt
$\frac{1}{4}$ cup tempera paint
1 $\frac{1}{4}$ cups water
1 tbs. oil

Method
1. Mix together the flour, salt, and powdered tempera paint.
2. Gradually add the water mixed with the oil.
3. Keep kneading the mixture as you add the liquid. Add more water if too stiff, more flour if too sticky.

BIBLE BOX (3 TO 6-YEAR-OLDS)

Goal

To provide opportunities for reinforcement of the story at home.

Description of Activity

Children help to make a Bible Box for home use (see Taking the Story Home below).

Materials

a large box with a lid
2 paper fasteners
a piece of string approximately 12" long
felt markers
glue
scissors
magazine pictures

Procedure

1. Describe the Bible Box and its purpose to each child. Explain that it will be kept at home and used there by the child and his/her family. Discuss the materials needed and the procedure for making the box.
2. The teacher or the child makes 2 small holes on the lid of the box approximately 6" apart. See diagram below:

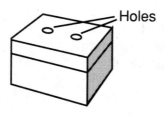
Holes

3. To make the handle, tie each end of the string around each of two paper fasteners. Push the fasteners through the small holes and open them. See diagram below:

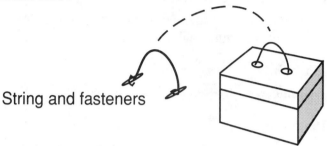

String and fasteners

4. Provide the child with felt markers, glue, scissors, and magazine pictures for decorating the box in a creative fashion.
5. Send the Bible Box home with a note to parents explaining that you will be sending suggestions for items to put in the box. If possible, include a length of brightly colored material when you send the box home.

Game Time

Goal

To help the children relate to the personalities in the story.

DO YOU KNOW ME? (3 AND 4-YEAR-OLDS)

Description of Activity

Children share their mental images of characters in the story through participation in a game.

Procedure

1. The teacher introduces the game and acts out a character or animal from the story.
2. Invite the children to guess the identity of the character or animal, but only after the acting out is finished.
3. The child who is the first to guess correctly takes a turn as actor.
4. Continue the game until all who wish to have had a turn.

GUESS WHO/WHAT I AM (5 AND 6-YEAR-OLDS)

Description of Activity

Children take turns describing a character or animal in the story while others guess who/what it is.

Materials

Procedure

1. Describe a character or animal in the story (for example, "I'm woolly, I have four legs, people get wool from me").
2. The children try to guess the identity of the person, animal, or thing being described.
3. The child who is the first to guess correctly takes a turn as leader while others again try to guess the identity of the character, animal, or thing being described.
4. Continue in this manner until all have had a turn or until interest in the game wanes.

TAKING THE STORY HOME

1. Send home a Bible Box with each child (made in school according to the instructions above). Include a length of brightly colored material for dramatic play. Suggest that parents add the following materials to the box: jewelry, scarves, puppets, sacks and packs of different dimensions, more lengths of colorful material, and other items of interest to the children. Children may also bring items home from school to add to the box. Encourage parents to review the story with the child, then initiate dramatic play using the materials in the box. Include friends and siblings whenever possible.
2. Send home a list of story starters for the children to complete. Examples follow:
    *   Many years ago Abraham and his wife Sarah . . .
    *   One day when Abraham was in the field with his sheep . . .
    *   Suddenly Abraham heard a voice saying . . .
    *   Abraham told Sarah what had happened to him in the field. He said, "Today . . ."

- Sarah was sad about leaving her home because . . .
- Sarah cried because . . .

3. Suggest to parents that they help their child make a book on the story. Give parents a list of materials needed (construction paper, felt markers or crayons, hole punch, a paper fastener). The child draws as many pictures as he/she wishes describing different aspects of the story. As the child draws, parents and child discuss the pictures and the story. Parents help the child to sequence the pictures according to the order of events in the story. Punch a hole in the upper left-hand corner of each picture. Secure the pages of the book together with a paper fastener (see diagram below). The child can then "read" the book to parents and other family members.

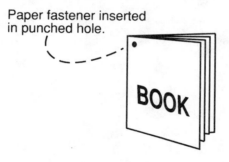

Paper fastener inserted in punched hole.

BOOK

CHAPTER 2

Abraham Receives Guests

BEFORE TELLING THE STORY

1. Provide background information by holding a preliminary discussion about tents. Encourage the children to share their knowledge about tents (shapes, materials, usage). Add any missing information to the children's comments.
2. Explain that in biblical times, most people lived in tents. Compare the tent to a sukkah in terms of structure, permanence, and portability. Compare the tent to a modern house in terms of physical structure, permanence, portability.
3. Show pictures of a variety of tents.
4. Bring a real tent into the classroom. As you set it up, discuss the material from which it is made, as well as its structure.

TELLING THE STORY

Abraham Receives Guests

Abraham sat in the doorway of his tent. Sarah relaxed inside. It was a very hot day. The sheep were resting, lizards hid under rocks, and birds were in their nests. Everything was quiet.

Suddenly Abraham looked up. He saw three men standing near his tent. He ran to them calling, "Welcome, welcome! Shalom, Shalom." The three men smiled.

Abraham pointed to a shady tree near his tent. "Please come and rest in the shade. I will get you some water to wash the sand off your tired feet. Then we'll have something to eat and drink."

Abraham rushed into the tent. "Sarah," he whispered, "hurry and bake your special bread for our guests. I will get butter and fresh milk." He dashed out to milk the goat while Sarah started mixing the dough. After the visitors washed and rested, Abraham served them the bread that Sarah had prepared, along with other good tasting food.

As they were eating, Abraham stood nearby. "Would you like some more bread? Something sweet, perhaps? Dates? Raisins?"

"You are very kind," said the three men. "You invited us to share your food even though you don't know us." Abraham felt good.

The men asked, "Where is your wife Sarah?"

"She's in the tent," said Abraham pointing in that direction.

Then the men said, "You have a good life here. It seems that you have everything you would ever want."

Abraham looked down. His face was sad. "Sarah and I have a very good life. We have a nice home, but we don't have everything. We don't have a child."

"Now we have something very important to tell you," said the men. "You will be surprised. Next year at this time, Sarah will give birth to a baby boy."

Abraham couldn't believe what he heard! Could it be possible? He wanted to tell Sarah the good news, but before he even had a chance to go into the tent, he heard laughter coming from that direction. It was Sarah. She stood in the doorway of the tent, laughing and laughing.

"Why is Sarah laughing?" asked the visitors.

"I am laughing because old women cannot have babies," said Sarah. "Abraham and I are very old. It would be unusual for us to have a baby now."

"Nothing is impossible for God," said one of the visitors. "You'll see — next year with God's help, you will be hugging your baby."

"Yes," whispered Abraham. "God has created everything. God will help us."

Then the visitors left. Abraham walked with them for a while to show them the way. He said good-bye and went back home.

It happened as the three guests had said. A year later Sarah had a baby.

"What a beautiful baby boy!" said Abraham with a big happy smile. "We'll give him a name at the baby naming ceremony when he's eight days old."

Abraham and his helpers prepared for the Brit Milah, the naming ceremony for boys. It was held on the eighth day after the baby was born. The baby was named Isaac because Abraham and Sarah remembered that Sarah had laughed when she learned that she would have a baby. Isaac means "laugh."

Abraham and Sarah took good care of Isaac. They watched him grow. He got bigger and bigger. They were a happy family.

When Isaac was big enough to drink from a cup, Sarah and Abraham had a party to celebrate. They were proud of the way Isaac had grown. Isaac felt very proud, too.

Questions on the Story
1. Why was Abraham friendly to the three visitors?
2. Why did Sarah prepare food for them?
3. Why was Abraham sad when he told the visitors that he and Sarah had no child?
4. What is a ceremony? Why did Sarah and Abraham have a ceremony after Isaac was born?
5. Why did Sarah and Abraham have a party when Isaac was able to drink from a cup?
6. Why did Sarah laugh? (5 and 6-year-olds)

THEMES IN THE STORY

Abraham and Sarah Extend Hospitality

Abraham and Sarah welcomed guests in a hospitable way and are role models for all of us. When you invite guests to class, be sure to mention Abraham's and Sarah's hospitality.

Bringing the Theme Closer
- Discuss the value of hospitality as shown by Abraham's efforts to make the three guests comfortable.
- Extend the discussion to include the children's attitudes and behaviors. Ask: How did Abraham and Sarah make their guests feel at home? How do we make guests feel at home in our classroom? What do we do to get ready for guests? How do your parents prepare for guests?

- After visitors to the class leave, ask: Were the guests happy? Were the preparations adequate?

Children Are Special to Parents

Isaac was truly a wanted child. Young children need to feel that they, too, are wanted.

Bringing the Theme Closer
- Were Abraham and Sarah anxious to have a baby? How do you know this?
- Why do you think they were so eager to have a baby?
- How do you think Abraham and Sarah felt when they heard God's promise that they would have a son?
- What are some things parents do with and for their babies?

CREATIVE FOLLOW UP

Retelling the Story

ROLE PLAY (3 AND 4-YEAR-OLDS)

Goals

To reinforce information acquired during the telling of the story.
To encourage children to imagine what life was like in Abraham's time.

Description of Activity

Children talk about story characters through the use of a prop box.

Materials

box filled with:
    pictures of sheep, trees, tent, camels, vegetation in arid lands
scarves
robes
sandals
sacks

Procedure

1. Fill a box with specific objects that can be used to encourage and stimulate dramatic play. Use the materials from this box to reinforce learning concepts through dramatic play.
2. Encourage the children to use any material in the prop box.
3. The teacher narrates the story.
4. Each child takes what he/she needs from the prop box for the part that he/she wishes to play.
5. The children interact as they interpret their parts.
6. Continue for no longer than ten minutes.

PICTURES (5 AND 6-YEAR-OLDS)

Goals

To reinforce information acquired during the telling of the story.
To encourage children to imagine what life was like in Abraham's time.
To identify some things we do today that are similar to things done in Abraham's time.

Description of Activity

Children tell their own version of the story through pictures.

Materials

paper
felt markers

Procedure

1. Have children create pictures based upon their own understanding of the story (examples of ideas are: Abraham welcoming guests, Sarah describing the guests to her friends, Sarah preparing food with her servants).
2. Have children share their pictures with a group of other children. Discuss similarities and differences between life in the time of Abraham and Sarah and life today.

Cooking

Goal

To gain knowledge of life styles in the land of Israel, ancient and modern.

MAKE A PITA AND ISRAELI SALAD (3 TO 6-YEAR-OLDS)

Description of Activity

Children make pita bread and an Israeli salad.

Materials

Ingredients and supplies for two recipes below

Procedure

1. Gather the ingredients for pita bread and for Israeli salad that are listed below.
2. Follow the instructions under "Method" for each recipe.

Pita – Israeli Flat Bread

Ingredients

 1 package active dry yeast
 $3/4$ cup warm water
 1 tsp. sugar
 2 cups bread flour
 1 tsp. salt
 oil

Supplies

 large bowl
 mixing spoon
 measuring cup
 measuring spoons
 board

Method

1. Dissolve yeast and sugar in warm water.
2. Stir in flour and salt; work into a dough.
3. Turn out dough onto a floured surface and knead until dough is smooth (about 8 minutes).
4. Place dough in greased bowl, turning the dough to grease the top. Cover and allow to rise in a warm place for about 45 minutes. (Make a warm place by setting the bowl in a pan of hot water. Place baking sheets over a hot water bath or in a warm oven.)
5. Turn out dough onto a floured surface. Punch down and knead slightly. Form into 8-10 small balls and roll to about $1/4$" rounds.

Place on slightly floured baking sheets. Brush with oil to prevent drying out. Allow to rise ¹/₂ hour in a warm place.

6. Bake on the bottom shelf in a preheated oven at 500 degrees until pitas are puffed and golden.

Note: Make a pocket in the pita and serve with a sandwich or salad filling or falafel (fried chickpea balls). Serve with butter or humus dip.

(Yield: Makes 8-10 small breads or five 6" circles)

Reprinted with permission from *Recipes and Jewish Cooking Experiences for Pre-School Children* by Marcia R. Kargon. Baltimore: Baltimore Board of Jewish Education, 1983.

Israeli Salad

Ingredients

green peppers
tomatoes
cucumbers
parsley
salad oil
lemon juice
salt
pepper

Supplies

knife
large bowl

Method

1. Cut equal amounts of the vegetables into small pieces (approximately ¹/₄" square.)
2. Combine the vegetables and add the other four ingredients to taste. Mix well and serve.

Building/Creating

Goals

To stimulate in the children the ability to imagine life in biblical times. To encourage the children to play actively in tents.

MAKE A TENT (3 AND 4-YEAR-OLDS)

Description of Activity

Children make and use a tent.

Materials

4 twin sheets
piece of rope

Procedure

1. Take two twin-size sheets and use them to cover the doorway to the classroom to give the impression of a tent.
2. Take two other sheets and drape them over ropes strung across the length and width of the room.
3. Encourage the children to eat, play, and entertain in the tent.

MAKE A TENT (5 AND 6-YEAR-OLDS)

Description of Activity

Children and teacher create experience stories and build mock tents.

Materials

4 twin-size sheets
piece of rope
experience chart
felt marker
fabric
paper
popsicle sticks

Procedure

1. Create experience stories with the children on:

a. why tents were important to Abraham and his family.
        b. why and when people use tents today.
2. A few children at a time can also build small "mock" tents out of fabric, paper, popsicle sticks, etc. Help the children as necessary. Share and discuss the tents.

Music and Dance

Goal

To reinforce mental images of the characters in the story.

SING AND SWAY (3 AND 4-YEAR-OLDS)

Description of Activity

Children dress up and move creatively to a song.

Materials

scarves
robes
tape recorder
song: "And Sarah Laughed" on the cassette tape *Bible People Songs* by Jeff Klepper

Procedure

1. Have children dress themselves in scarves and robes to look the way they think Sarah and Abraham looked.
2. As "And Sarah Laughed" is played and the verse is sung, the boys move to the music as they think Abraham would have moved.
3. As the chorus is sung, the boys sit down and the girls move to the music and sing the "Ha-ha-ha."

SING ALONG – WITH MASKS (5 AND 6-YEAR-OLDS)

Description of Activity

Children move to a song using masks.

Materials

construction paper
felt markers
yarn
glue
scissors
tape recorder
song: "And Sarah Laughed" on the cassette tape *Bible People Songs*
    by Jeff Klepper

Procedure

1. Each child draws a face on construction paper. Masks may be decorated with markers, and yarn glued on for hair.
2. As "And Sarah Laughed" is played and the verse is sung, children hold their Abraham faces in front of their own and sing along.
3. As the chorus is sung, children hold their Sarah faces in front of their own and sing along.

TAKING THE STORY HOME

1. Ask parents to tell their children how long they were waiting for a child before they had one, how they prepared for the new baby, and how very special each child is to them.
2. Send home ideas for story starters for children to complete. Examples follow:
   • When Abraham saw the three men standing near his tent, he . . .
   • Abraham rushed into the tent and said, "Sarah . . ."
   • The men said, "We have something very important to tell you. . . ."
   • Sarah said, "I am laughing because . . ."

CHAPTER 3

A Wife for Isaac

BEFORE TELLING THE STORY

1. In order to help children understand the significance of Rebecca's helpfulness at the well, provide the children with some background on wells. The information should include how wells are built, where well water comes from, how the water is drawn up from the well.
2. Contrast the way we get water in our homes today with the method of drawing water from a well.

TELLING THE STORY

Abraham and Eliezer

Abraham, Sarah, and Isaac lived in the land of Canaan. They had a good life there. Weeks passed. Months passed. Years and more years passed. Abraham and Sarah were proud of Isaac. They loved him very much. But Abraham and Sarah were both very old. Sarah was 127 years old when she died. Isaac missed his mother. He thought about her a lot.

Abraham also thought of Sarah. He looked back over his life. "I have had a good life. I own land and sheep and goats and camels and donkeys. I have many people working for me. God has made me a rich man. I feel unhappy, though, that my son Isaac is not yet married. I wish he had a wife to keep him company and to give me grandchildren."

Abraham worried about a wife for Isaac for a very long time. At last, he came up with a plan. He called his servant Eliezer to his tent. "Eliezer, I want you to go back to the country from which I came. Visit my relatives there, my brother and his children and grandchildren. Find out if there is a young woman there who would make a good wife for Isaac. Isaac must not marry someone from the land of Canaan where we now live. God will help you find the right person."

Eliezer thought for a few moments. He asked, "What should I do if I find someone there for Isaac to marry, but she doesn't want to come back here? Should I take Isaac to her?"

"No," answered Abraham, "never take Isaac from here. God has said that I am to stay in the land of Canaan with my family. If you find someone who will not live here, she is not the right person for Isaac. But don't worry, God will help you."

Eliezer said, "Abraham, you are a good man. You have been kind to me. I will do as you wish. I will bring back the right woman for Isaac to marry."

Eliezer hurried to pack. He took food and water for the long trip. He took many gifts for Abraham's family in Haran. Most important of all, he took ten of Abraham's camels as gifts. He also took some men to help him along the way. At last, he was ready to leave.

Questions on the Story

1. Will Eliezer find a suitable bride for Isaac? Why do you think so?
2. Do you think camels were good gifts for Eliezer to bring? Why or why not? Do you think camels would be good gifts today? Why or why not?

Eliezer Meets Rebecca

Eliezer and the camels walked for a long, long time. They stopped sometimes to eat, sometimes to drink water, sometimes to rest. Eliezer knew that he was doing something very important. Even though he was tired, he kept going.

At last, he saw a group of people in the distance. They were drawing water from a well. As Eliezer came closer to the group, he wondered, "How will I find the right girl for Isaac?" Then he prayed to God for help. He said to himself, "I will ask a young girl for water. I hope she will give me a drink, and also offer water to my camels. Maybe she will be the right one for Isaac to marry."

Even before Eliezer finished praying, a pretty young girl came to the well. She carried a pitcher on her shoulder. Eliezer watched her as she drew water from the well. He ran to meet her. "I am so thirsty," he said. "Might I have a little water?" The girl smiled and answered, "Please drink, and then I will draw water for your camels." And that was what she did.

Eliezer was so happy. He thought, "She is kind and pretty! Maybe she will be the wife for Isaac."

It was good to have a cold drink. "I was very thirsty!" Eliezer said. "You have been very kind. Please take this golden ring and these two bracelets as a gift from us."

Rebecca was surprised, but pleased with the gifts. "Thank you, thank you," she said as she put them on.

Eliezer was curious. "What is your name and your family's name?" he asked. The girl answered, "My name is Rebecca and my parent is Bethuel." When Eliezer heard this, he thought, "This girl is the daughter of Abraham's relative Bethuel." Then Eliezer asked, "Is there a place for me and for the camels to sleep tonight?" We have lots of room at my house," answered Rebecca.

Eliezer was really excited now. "God has led me to Isaac's wife!" he thought. "She is kind and sweet and generous." He was so thrilled that he said a prayer of thanks to God right then and there.

Questions on the Story
1. Do you think Eliezer will choose Rebecca as a bride for Isaac? Why?
2. Why did Rebecca take a gift from someone she didn't know? Do you take gifts from strangers? Why not?
3. "Drawing water" is a term that is used for getting water from a well. How do we talk about getting water from a faucet? (5 and 6-year-olds)

Rebecca and Her Family

Rebecca ran home. She called, "We have guests. They've come from far away. I told them that they can stay with us. Is that all right?"

"Of course, Rebecca," said Bethuel, "but let's make room for them." They made room for the guests. Then Rebecca's brother Laban went to greet the guests. "Welcome to our home," he said. "We have food for you all and a place for your camels."

Eliezer said, "Thank you for your kindness, but I must first tell you why I am here." Eliezer told them about Abraham's life in

Canaan and about Sarah and Isaac. He told them that he came to Haran to find a wife for Isaac. He said, "God has helped me to find a wife for Isaac so that I can bring her back to Canaan for the marriage. Rebecca was very kind and generous to us at the well. God has led me to her." Eliezer, Bethuel, and Laban talked for a very long time.

At last, Bethuel said, "You are right. God has led you to Rebecca. If she agrees to go with you to marry Isaac, she may do so."

Then Rebecca's mother and father spoke with her. "We want to do what God wants of us, yet you must decide whether or not to marry Isaac. Now we will eat and drink and rest for the night."

Rebecca thought and thought. She knew that if she married Isaac, she would live far away from her family. She wondered, "When will I see them again? Will I like Isaac? What will my new home be like?" She knew that she would be going to the home of relatives. She knew that her family wanted her to go there. She thought and thought until the next day. Then she decided. "I will go to the land of Canaan to marry Isaac!"

Eliezer was happy. He gave presents of silver, gold, and cloth to Rebecca and to everyone in the family.

Questions on the Story

1. What did Rebecca do that made Eliezer like her so much?
2. What do you think Rebecca should have done? Should she leave her home to marry Isaac? Why or why not?
3. What do you think would have happened if Rebecca had decided not to leave her home? (5 and 6-year-olds)

Back to Canaan

Early the next day Eliezer started preparing to return to Canaan. He could hardly wait to tell Abraham and Isaac the good news. He shouted with joy to his men, "Pack your things and get the camels ready for the long trip back."

Rebecca's mother helped her get her things together. Rebecca wondered, "What does it look like in the land of Canaan? What does Isaac look like? Will I be glad to be his wife?" She thought these thoughts as she left her family. She thought them as she and her servants rode on donkeys behind Eliezer. She wondered and wondered.

One afternoon Eliezer shouted, "Look! Someone is coming." Rebecca looked into the distance and asked, "Who is that?" "It's Isaac," smiled Eliezer, "he has come to meet us. Now we're very close to home."

Rebecca was excited, but she didn't say anything. She sat still and covered her face with a veil as Isaac came closer. At last she could see his face. She liked the way he looked. She knew that she would like her new husband and her new home. She was content that she had decided to marry Isaac.

Eliezer told Isaac about how he met Rebecca and her family in Haran. Isaac liked Rebecca very much. He was thankful that God had helped Eliezer find a wife for him.

Questions on the Story

1. What did Rebecca think about when she was getting ready to travel to Canaan where she would start a new life?
2. Do you think Isaac liked Rebecca when he first saw her?
3. Why do you think Rebecca wore a veil over her face? (5 and 6-year-olds)
4. Why do you think Abraham sent Eliezer to look for a wife for Isaac instead of going himself or sending Isaac? (5 and 6-year-olds)

THEMES IN THE STORY

Eliezer's Plan and His Faith in God

Eliezer had a plan that was based on his faith that God would help him find a wife for Isaac.

Bringing the Theme Closer

- Develop a conversation about the details of Eliezer's plans for his trip and the ways he expressed his faith that God would help him.

- Extend the discussion to deal with the children's plans and their expectations. Ask: What were Eliezer's hopes and plans? Why did Eliezer pray to God? How did God help Eliezer? If you were Eliezer and Abraham asked you to find a wife for Isaac, what would you do?

The Interaction Between Eliezer and Rebecca

The interaction between Eliezer and Rebecca is one of the most interesting elements in this story.

Bringing the Theme Closer
- How did Rebecca know that Eliezer was thirsty.
- How did Rebecca know that Eliezer was not from Haran? (5 and 6-year-olds)

Rebecca's Good Deeds

Rebecca's good deeds emphasized the fact that she was helpful even when requests were not made of her.

Bringing the Theme Closer
- Focus your discussion on Rebecca's good deeds, her character, and her feelings while she was helping Eliezer, his men, and his camels.

Bethuel's Family Receives Guests

Bethuel and his family were good hosts.

Bringing the Theme Closer
- Discuss the ways that Rebecca's family were good hosts. Ask: What did Rebecca do? What did Laban do? What did her parents do?
- Consider the feelings of a guest. What did Eliezer think when he received such warm hospitality?
- What would Eliezer have done if Rebecca had not invited him to stay with her family?
- There is someone else we learned about who invited a guest to his home. Who was it? What was his story? Did he receive his guest in the same way as Bethuel?

• Abraham and Bethuel invited strangers to their home. Did they do the right thing? Why? How do people feel when they are guests? When they are hosts? Do you invite strangers to your home? (Emphasize that our parents help us to decide when to invite strangers into our homes.)

CREATIVE FOLLOW UP

Retelling the Story

Goals

To develop an understanding of the important characters in the story.
To understand the sequence of events.
To encourage communication among the children.

PAPER PLATE PUPPETS (3 AND 4-YEAR-OLDS)

Description of Activity

Children communicate with their peers through the use of puppets.

Materials

paper plates
tongue depressors
felt markers or crayons
pieces of yarn
scissors
glue
stapler

Procedure

1. Gather 3 or 4 children together and review the story.
2. Discuss the characters and animals in the story.
3. Show the children a blank paper plate with a tongue depressor handle stapled onto it. Ask for ideas on designing the plate as a puppet.
4. Provide the materials at easy access and encourage the children to begin creating the puppets. While they work on their puppets, sit with the children and discuss the characters and animals in the story.
5. Use the puppets for role plays in the small groups and later before the entire class.

PAPER BAG PUPPETS (5 AND 6-YEAR-OLDS)

Description of Activity

Children create puppets based on their own mental images of the characters.

Materials

paper lunch bags
newspaper
fabric scraps
cotton balls
buttons
ribbon
yarn and string
seeds or noodles
pipe cleaners
feathers
straws or toothpicks
glue
scissors

Procedure

1. Gather 3 to 6 children together and review the story.
2. Discuss the characters and animals in the story.
3. Show the children a blank paper bag. Stuff it with crumpled newspaper. Tie a string around the bottom of the bag. Ask the children for ideas for decorating it.
4. Provide the materials at easy access and encourage children to begin creating the puppets. While they are working on the puppets, sit with them and discuss the characters and animals in the story.
5. The children can use the puppets to dramatize the characters for their small group and later for the entire class.

Planning Special Events

Goal

To help children understand the purposes and benefits of making a plan before acting as Eliezer did.

MAKE A PLAN FOR A DAY (3 AND 4-YEAR-OLDS)

Description of Project

Children make a plan for one day.

Materials

experience chart
felt marker

Procedure

1. During opening circle the teacher describes a plan for the day.
2. The teacher then asks the children to list the day's activities in order as he/she transcribes them onto an experience chart.
3. On the experience chart, list specific jobs for each child.
4. Assure children that every child's name is listed on the experience chart and that each will be responsible for an activity and/or a job during the day.
5. Before dismissal, review the chart with the children to see whether or not the plan was carried out.

MAKE A CLASS PLAN (5 AND 6-YEAR-OLDS)

Description of Activity

Children discuss special events through the use of an experience chart, then made a plan as Eliezer did.

Materials

newsprint paper
felt marker

Procedure

1. Discuss with the children the elements of Eliezer's plan to go to Haran and find a bride for Isaac. Emphasize that he first needed to organize a caravan for the long journey, that he took gifts along, and that he prayed for God's help before he arrived at the well.
2. On the first day of a new month, discuss the events in the month to come (i.e., birthdays, holidays, class trips, visitors to the class, etc.).
3. Record this schedule of events in chronological order on an experience chart.

4. As each event approaches, involve children in the planning of it. Record each plan on a separate experience chart.
5. After it is over, evaluate each event. Review the plan by going over the experience chart. Discuss the implementation of the plan. Did everyone do his/her job? Was the schedule adhered to? Was the event successful? Could the plan have been improved? If so, how? Refer back to Eliezer's plan. Was it well thought out? Did he stick to it? Was it successful?

Science

Goal

To help children understand how people in ancient times got water.

MAKE A WELL (3 AND 4-YEAR-OLDS)

Description of Activity

Children make a well.

Materials

large box filled with sand
low table
2 buckets, one fitting inside the other
string
water

Procedure

1. Fill a large box with sand and place it on a table low enough to make it accessible to the children.
2. Dig out the central area of the box and place a bucket securely into the sand. The top of the bucket should be at the height of the sand.
3. Fill the bucket approximately half full of water.
4. Tie a string around the handle of the smaller bucket.
5. Lower the smaller bucket into the larger one and scoop up water.
6. Raise the smaller bucket with the string.

MAKE A WELL (5 AND 6-YEAR-OLDS)

Description of Activity
Children make and use a well.

Materials
very large bucket
pulley
small pail
rope
water
felt marker

Procedure
1. Draw lines on the outside of a very large bucket to give the impression of a stone wall.
2. Attach a pulley to the handle above the bucket.
3. Tie a rope to a small pail.
4. Attach the rope to the pulley so that the pail can be drawn up and down.
5. Put water in the "well" and draw it up in the small pail.

TAKING THE STORY HOME

1. Encourage parents to discuss planning with their child. Share with parents how planning plays an important role in this story and in our daily lives. Elements to include in this discussion: Eliezer made a plan for his trip because of the importance of his task; his plan helped to make him successful; people who learn to make plans are usually happier with the way things work out for them than those who don't make plans. Encourage parents to discuss the plans for the week with their child. During the discussion parents can record the plans on paper. Suggest that the child create drawings to correspond with the plans. These drawings can then be collated into an album entitled "My Plans."
2. Parents can discuss with their child the differences between how people obtained water in ancient times and how we get it today. Which way is easier? Which way is better? Why?
3. Send home a list of story starters for the children to complete. Examples follow:

- Abraham was unhappy because . . .
- Abraham said to Eliezer, "Eliezer, I need you to go to the country from which I came so that you can . . . "
- Eliezer liked Rebecca because . . .
- Eliezer and his camels didn't have to worry about having a place to stay because . . .

CHAPTER 4

Jacob and Esau

BEFORE TELLING THE STORY

1. Involve children in a discussion about family relationships. Read age appropriate books on this topic. Some suggestions are: *Billy and Our New Baby* by Helen S. Arnstein (3 to 6-year-olds), *Little New Angel* by Sadie Rose Weilerstein (5 and 6-year-olds), *No Time for Me* by John Barrett (5 and 6-year-olds), *Matthew and His Dad* by Arlene Alda (3 to 6-year-olds).
2. To reinforce the continuity between the Bible stories, refer back to Isaac's earlier years. Discuss specifically Abraham's concerns about a wife for Isaac, Eliezer's journey to find a suitable bride for Isaac, and the first encounter of Isaac and Rebecca.

TELLING THE STORY

God's Promise

Isaac and Rebecca got married and had a home in Canaan. Things were very good for them. There was one very, very important thing, though, that Isaac and Rebecca didn't have. They thought about it all the time.

One day Rebecca said to Isaac, "Our home has so many good things. We are rich. Yet, I am miserable. We do not have children. Who will take care of our land and our animals when we are old?"

Isaac was miserable, too. He prayed to God for help. He prayed and prayed with all his heart. He hoped God would listen to his prayers.

Many days and weeks and months passed. Then one day something wonderful happened. Rebecca felt something move inside of her. "It's nothing," she thought at first. But it moved again and again.

"Isaac, I feel something moving inside of me," she said. She and Isaac looked at each other. Their eyes sparkled with happiness. They hugged each other and laughed out loud because they knew that Rebecca was going to have a baby.

Rebecca's womb grew bigger and bigger. She could feel something jumping inside of her. She wondered "What is happening in my womb? It feels so strange."

Rebecca was worried. She prayed to God, "What is moving in my womb so strongly?"

"Don't worry," God said to Rebecca. "There are two babies there – twin sons. Your babies will be born peacefully. They will grow up and marry. They will have many children and grandchildren and great-grandchildren. One son will be stronger than the other. Two leaders will come from you, two very different leaders. Each one will be a great leader, but the land of Canaan will go to the younger son and to his family."

Rebecca listened carefully. Then God said, "I will bless your sons."

When Isaac returned from the fields, Rebecca ran to him and said, "Isaac, Isaac, we're going to have twin sons. I prayed to God and that was what God told me."

Isaac hugged Rebecca and together they waited for the twins to be born.

Questions on the Story

1. Why were Isaac and Rebecca miserable when things were so very good for them?
2. Why did Isaac and Rebecca want so much to have children? (5 and 6-year-olds)
3. Why was Rebecca worried when she felt something inside of her jumping so strongly?
4. What do you think Isaac said when he learned that he and Rebecca were going to have twins? (5 and 6-year-olds)
5. What did God tell Rebecca about her twin sons?
6. Do you remember someone else in the Bible who wanted children? Who was that? What happened? How did Sarah and Abraham feel when Isaac was born? (5 and 6 year olds)

The Twins

Finally, the big day came. The first baby born had a lot of hair. The second baby was born holding onto the heel of his brother. His skin was smooth. The twins looked very different.

Isaac and Rebecca were overjoyed. They prayed. "Thank you, God, for listening to our prayers. We are fortunate."

"Now we should name the babies," said Rebecca. "Let us call the oldest son Esau."

"Let us call the younger one Jacob," said Isaac, "because he held onto his brother's heel at birth." Isaac and Rebecca were happy with their family.

The years passed. The boys grew bigger. Esau was big and strong. He had lots of hair on his body. Esau loved to play wild games. He was a good hunter. Jacob loved quiet, gentle games. He liked to stay at home. The brothers were very, very different.

Esau was very proud that he was born first. Jacob wished that he had been born first.

Questions on the Story

1. What did Esau look like? What kind of boy was he? What did he like to do?
2. What did Jacob look like? What kind of boy was he? What did he like to do?
3. Why do you think Jacob wished that he had been born first?

The Birthright

Years passed and the boys became men. One day Esau went out hunting for animals. Jacob stayed home. He liked to cook.

When Esau finally returned from hunting, he was tired, sweaty, and hungry. As he came into the tent, he found Jacob cooking a stew of red lentil beans.

"How good the food smells," said Esau. "I am very hungry. Jacob, give me some of that red stuff."

Jacob saw how exhausted and hungry his brother was. He thought for a moment. Then he said, "I'll gladly give you some of this stew if you give me your birthright. I want everyone to treat me as though I was born first."

Esau was so hungry, he couldn't stand it. "Take it," he said. "I don't need the birthright now." Then he took the stew and ate it as fast as he could. He felt good.

Questions on the Story

1. What do you think about what Jacob did to get Esau's birthright? What Esau did?
2. What would you have done if you were Jacob? If you were Esau? (5 and 6-year-olds)
3. What is a birthright? (Explain the idea that older children in a family frequently help the younger ones and that the oldest in the family frequently is the one to assume family responsibilities.) (5 and 6-yar-olds)

The Twins Grow Up

Many years passed. The brothers had grown up. Esau got married. He had sons and daughters. He had a big family. Jacob was not married yet.

Rebecca wondered about what God had told her when she was pregnant. She remembered that God had said that her younger son would be a greater leader than her older son. She wondered when it would happen. She wondered how it would happen.

Isaac was an old man. He could not see well. He thought, "I don't know how much longer I will live. When I die my children will take my place. I must bless them before I die."

The next morning Isaac called Esau to come to him. "Listen, my son. I am very old. I want to bless you now."

Esau was thrilled. He thought, "Father will bless me. This will make me more important than Jacob. Then Jacob will have to do whatever I tell him to do."

Isaac said, "Go to the field with your bow and arrows and hunt an animal. Cook it for me the way I like it. Then I will eat it and afterwards I will bless you." When he heard this, Esau ran to get his bow and arrows.

Rebecca was listening nearby as Isaac talked to Esau. She was angry. She thought, "I wonder why Isaac promised the blessing to Esau. He knows that God promised me that Jacob would receive the blessing. Maybe he forgot. Then she said to herself, "I'll have to do something to make sure that Isaac doesn't give the blessing to Esau."

Rebecca had an idea. She said to Jacob, "I heard your father talking to Esau. He asked Esau to hunt an animal for him and then to cook it. Father promised that after he finishes eating the food, he will bless Esau so that Esau will be in charge after Isaac dies. Before you and Esau were born, God promised me that you would be the one to get the blessing. Your father must have forgotten. Now, Jacob, do as I tell you. Bring me two nice goats. I'll prepare them the way Isaac likes. When the food is ready, you will bring it to him. Then your father will bless you instead of Esau."

Jacob was confused. "Mother," he said, "how can I tell father that I'm Esau when I'm not Esau?"

"Don't worry," said Rebecca. "God wants you to get the blessing. So do as I tell you." Jacob did as his mother said.

Questions on the Story

1. What did Isaac ask Esau to bring him?
2. Why did Jacob pretend to be Esau?
3. What did Rebecca ask Jacob to do?

The Blessing

"Come now and put on these clothes," Rebecca said to Jacob. She gave him some of Esau's clothing.

Jacob said, "I don't want to wear Esau's clothes. They are too big for me."

"Don't worry," said Rebecca. "I've thought of everything. I'll make them fit."

After Jacob dressed in Esau's clothing, Rebecca wrapped hairy goat skin on Jacob's hands and neck. Then he took the tray with the food on it that Rebecca had prepared. He went into his father's tent. The inside of the tent was a little dark. He came close to his father and said, "Father, I brought you the food that you asked for."

Isaac listened to the voice and asked, "Who are you, my son?" Jacob was quiet for a moment. Then he answered in a quiet voice, "I am Esau, your older son. I did what you asked. I brought you food so that you would eat and then bless me."

"Come near so that I can feel you and know that you are Esau," said Isaac.

Slowly, very slowly, Jacob walked to Isaac. He stretched out his hands so that Isaac could touch them. "Your hands are hairy like those of Esau." Isaac said. "Bring me the food that you prepared, so that I can eat it and then I will bless you." Jacob put the food in front of Isaac. Isaac ate it. It was delicious.

Isaac said, "Come near me and kiss me." Jacob walked to Isaac and kissed him. Isaac put his hands on his son's head and blessed him. He said, "God will bless you and give you good things – rain to water the fields, good soil to grow crops, vegetables and fruits. You will have many cattle, sheep, and goats. You will be in charge after I die." When Isaac was finished, Jacob thanked him and kissed him.

As soon as Jacob left, Esau arrived. He said in a loud voice, "Father, look at the wonderful food I prepared for you."

Isaac was confused. "Who are you?" he asked.

"I'm Esau, your older son." said Esau.

"But someone just left. He brought me food and I blessed him," Isaac said.

"Who was that?" asked Esau.

"Your brother Jacob came to me and said that he was Esau. I thought it was you, so I blessed him."

Esau was very angry. "Jacob took my birthright." (He had forgotten that he had given Jacob the birthright a long time ago.) He began to sob and cry.

"Father, do you have only one blessing? Bless me, too," Esau said. Isaac felt Esau's sadness and anger, but he understood that it was God's will that Jacob should receive the blessing.

"I will bless you with a different blessing," he said to Esau. "You will raise many crops, fruits, and vegetables and there will be enough rain to water the land. But, you will use the sword – you will be a hunter. Your brother Jacob will be in charge here after I die. You will have to listen to him."

Esau thanked his father for the blessing. Then he left the tent and went home.

Questions on the Story

1. How did Jacob fool his father?
2. When Jacob said that he was Esau, what did Isaac do?
3. What did Esau do when he learned that Jacob had received his blessing?
4. What do you think will happen when Jacob and Esau meet again?
5. Why did Esau forget that he had sold his birthright to Jacob? (5 and 6-year-olds)

Esau Is Angry

Esau was very angry with Jacob because of the blessing. He didn't know that Rebecca had told Jacob to get the blessing. He didn't know that Jacob had done so because it was what God wanted. He thought only that Jacob had tricked him.

Rebecca was afraid that Esau would try to hurt Jacob. She said to Jacob, "Your brother Esau is furious with you because your father blessed you. Listen to me and do as I say. Take some clothes and food for a trip and go to the house of my brother Laban in Haran. Uncle Laban will be happy to have you stay in his house for a while."

Jacob was upset. "I want to stay here with you and father." he said, "I don't want to go far away to Laban's house."

"Stay with Uncle Laban for a little while until Esau calms down. When I see that he is no longer angry, I will send for you to come back home."

"I'll stay here and hide from Esau," said Jacob.

Rebecca smiled. "You can't hide from Esau. Esau is a hunter. He will find you. I don't want either of my sons to be hurt." Jacob did as his mother said, but he was unhappy and worried.

Rebecca told Isaac that Jacob was preparing to leave. Isaac called Jacob to him and blessed him again. "You are going to the land of Haran from which your mother comes," said Isaac. "Meet a nice girl there. Marry her and have a family. Whenever you can, return to your land, to Canaan. God gave this land to Abraham, my father, and to me. Someday it will be your land, too."

Jacob left just before the sun came up. It was still dark outside.

Questions on the Story:

1. Was Jacob excited or worried about going to Haran?
2. Did Jacob really fool Isaac by dressing up as Esau?
3. Why was Esau so angry with Jacob? Did he forget that he had sold his birthright? (5 and 6-year-olds)

THEMES IN THE STORY

Isaac and Rebecca Were Shepherds

The major occupation of our ancestors was tending sheep. Isaac and Rebecca were shepherds like their parents before them.

Bringing the Theme Closer
- Discuss some aspects of shepherding with the children (e.g., caring for animals, being alone for long periods of time, coping with difficult weather).
- If possible, visit a sheep farm. Feel sheared wool and watch the carding, spinning, and wool dyeing process.
- Set up a display of wool in the Bible corner. Include photos of sheep and of the process of preparing the wool. Encourage the children to bring in woolen objects to display in the Bible corner.

Children Are Born to Isaac and Rebecca

In this story, Isaac and Rebecca long for a child. They are blessed with twins.

Bringing the Theme Closer
- Do you remember another story about someone who very much wanted a baby?
- Do you think Isaac and Rebecca were surprised when twins were born instead of one child? When was your last surprise? What was it?
- How do children make their parents happy?
- How do you make your parents happy? How can you tell when you do?

The Twins

In this story twins are mentioned for the first time. Sibling rivalry is also related to this theme.

Bringing the Theme Closer
- Discuss twins. Ask the children if they know any twins. Do all twins look alike? Do they act alike? In what ways do they look or act different from each other?
- Were your parents excited when you were born?
- Would you like to have a twin? Why?
- Did Rebecca think it would be fun to have twins? (5 and 6-year-olds)
- Do you know twins? In what way are they alike? In what ways are they different?
- Are you similar or different from your brother or sister? In what ways?
- Esau and Jacob were alike in some ways and different in others. In what ways were they alike? In what ways were they different? (5 and 6-year-olds)
- What things did Esau and Jacob do together? What things would they want to do alone? (5 and 6-year-olds)
- What can brothers and sisters do together?
- How can you help your baby brother or sister?
- Did you ever have an argument with your brother or sister? What happened? What happened after the argument was finished?
- Is it a good idea to go away for a while from the person you've argued with? Why? What can happen when you get back together with that person?

Isaac Blessed Jacob and Esau

The blessing of children by parents is mentioned frequently in the Bible. For example, Jacob blessed his sons and he blessed Joseph's sons.

Bringing the Theme Closer
- Discuss blessings, what they mean, and why. When do we say them and what do we say?
- Discuss the tradition of parents blessing their children before Shabbat on Friday evening. Bless the children as a group during the class preparation for a pre-Shabbat party.
- Help the children deal with the fact that Rebecca encouraged Jacob to deceive his father. Ask: Why was Esau chosen by Isaac to receive the blessing? Why did Isaac bless Jacob instead of Esau? Why did Rebecca want Jacob to receive the blessing?
- How did Jacob feel when pretending to be Esau? (5 and 6-year-olds)
- How did Esau feel when he found that Jacob has received his blessing? How do you feel when someone gets something that belongs to you? (5 and 6-year-olds)

Rebecca Is a Multifaceted Personality

Rebecca is a major character who influences the course of this story.

Bringing the Theme Closer
- Talk with the children about Rebecca at various stages of her life. Help them to develop a mental image of her as a young woman at the well, as Isaac's wife, as the mother of twins, as the mother who helped Jacob receive the blessing, as the mother who helped Jacob run away from his angry brother.
- Ask: Was Rebecca a nice person? How do you know that? Was she a smart person? Why do you or don't you think so? Emphasize that Rebecca was the only person in this story to have heard God's voice.

CREATIVE FOLLOW UP

Retelling the Story

Goals

To reinforce information acquired during the telling of the story.
To help the children sequence the events of the story.
To encourage the children to imagine what life was like in the time of Jacob's youth.

MAGIC BOX (3 AND 4-YEAR-OLDS)

Description of Activity

Using the pictures in the Magic Box, children play a guessing game.

Materials

box containing pictures of sheep, goats, tent, robe
stool or chair

Procedure

1. Form a group of 3 to 4 children while other children are involved in free choice activities.
2. Give each child a turn picking a picture from the Magic Box. (Be sure the other children can't see the picture.)
3. The child can imitate the animal or object or talk about it without identifying it.
4. The other children guess the name of the animal or object and discuss how it fits into the story of Jacob and Esau.
5. Repeat this procedure in small groups with other children until all who wish to participate have done so.

MAGIC BOX (5 AND 6-YEAR-OLDS)

Description of Activity

Using the pictures in the Magic Box, children retell the story.

Materials

box containing pictures of a tent, a pot, a robe, a sheep skin
stool or chair

Procedure

1. After the story has been told, seat the children in a circle. Place the box on the stool/chair on one side of the circle. Tell the children it is a magic box.
2. Designate one child to pick a picture from the box.
3. The child shows the picture to the group, reads the label, and talks about that object as it is mentioned in the story.
4. Another child is then chosen to pick a picture from the box.
5. Continue in this way until all the pictures have been used, until each of the children has had a turn, or until the interest of the children wanes.
6. Repeat this activity on subsequent occasions so that each child can have a turn to reach into the Magic Box.

Dramatic Play

Goals

To determine how much children remember about the story.
To help children internalize the story.

ROLE PLAY (3 AND 4-YEAR-OLDS)

Description of Activity

Children role play the story with props.

Materials

robes
stuffed animals (sheep, goat)

Procedure

1. Tell the story with the children's help.

2. Put the materials in a place that is easily accessible to the children.
3. Encourage several children to take props and role play parts of the story.
4. Continue the role play during the free play time for several days or wait a day or two and then continue.
5. Have a group of children do improvisations for the class during circle time.

ROLE PLAY (5 AND 6-YEAR-OLDS)

Description of Activity

Children role play the story with props, then comment on an experience chart.

Materials

robes
stuffed animals (sheep, goat)
pot
sheepskin
pictures of tents, animals, desert areas (see picture section at the end of this book)
newsprint paper
felt marker

Procedure

1. Tell the story with the children's help.
2. Put materials (except experience chart) in a place that is easily accessible to the children.
3. Encourage several children to take props and to role play parts of the story.
4. Continue this activity for several days during the free play time. Then elicit from the children commments about the story and write these down on the experience chart. Continue using the experience chart for several days.
5. The children and the teacher "read" the experience chart together.

Building/Creating

Goal

To enable children to reinforce their mental images of the story.

MAKE A MOCK TENT (3 AND 4-YEAR-OLDS)

Description of Activity

Children build mock tents out of blocks and fabric.

Materials

wooden blocks
pieces of fabric of different sizes
small play people

Procedure

1. Display pictures of tents near the block center.
2. Sit with a group of children and begin to build a tent out of blocks and fabric pieces.
3. Encourage the children to build alongside of you.
4. Place the play people in the tent.

MAKE A MOCK TENT (5 AND 6-YEAR-OLDS)

Description of Activity

Children create mock tents out of a variety of materials.

Materials

fabric
construction paper
popsicle sticks
glue
scissors

Procedure

1. Display pictures of tents near an art table. On the table place a variety of materials for making mock tents.
2. Bring a group of 4-6 children together to discuss tents and their characteristics with the children, while drawing their attention to the pictures on display.
3. Encourage the children to begin creating their own mock tents. Stay on the sidelines, but remain available for assistance as needed.
4. Encourage other groups of children to participate in this project later during the day or on another day.
5. When all those who wish to create a mock tent have had the opportunity to do so, display the tents on a table in the Bible corner and later take them home. Let children share their creations during circle time, noting the similarities and differences between them.

TAKING THE STORY HOME

1. Send home a variety of pictures of objects and animals that appear in the story. Suggest that parents ask their child to identify the pictures and tell the story. Ask that other family members also participate in the activity.
2. Play a Bible character charade game. Each family member has a few minutes to act out a character from this story. The person who guesses correctly becomes the actor.
3. Send home a list of story starters for children to complete. Examples follow:

   • When Isaac heard that Rebecca was going to have a baby, he . . .
   • When Esau asked for some stew, Jacob . . .
   • After hearing that Isaac was going to bless Esau, Rebecca told Jacob to . . .
   • When Jacob and Esau meet again, they will . . .
   • When Jacob left for Haran, Isaac told him to . . .

CHAPTER 5

Jacob's Journey

BEFORE TELLING THE STORY

1. Discuss the importance of water and conservation of water in the time of the Patriarchs. Compare with issues of water conservation today.
2. Review the events preceding Jacob's flight. Ask the children: Do you think Jacob should have run away? What else could Jacob have done? What did Jacob do to prepare for his departure?

TELLING THE STORY

Leaving Home

Jacob got up early in the morning. Everyone was sleeping. He left the house quietly and quickly so that his brother Esau would not hear him. It was still dark outside.

He took food and extra clothes for the trip to Laban's house in Haran. It would take many days to get there.

Jacob felt terrible. "I'm leaving my home for a country that's far away. I don't know when I'll see my family again. If only Esau would forgive me. Then I could go back home. I'll probably need to stay in Haran for a long time." Jacob traveled for many hours. He was getting very tired. The trip was long. He was far from home.

"Maybe I should stop and rest for a while," he thought. When he found a place to rest, he took out his food, sat on the ground, and ate. As he ate, he yawned and stretched. "Oh, I'm so tired. My eyes are starting to close."

"This ground is very hard," Jacob thought. "I need a small pillow for my head." He looked all around. He found a stone. He lay down on the ground with his head on the stone. He looked at the sky. The stars were sparkling and the moon was shining. His eyes closed and he fell fast asleep.

As Jacob slept he had a dream. In his dream he saw a very tall ladder. It went from the ground up to the sky. Angels of God went up and down the ladder – from the ground to the sky and from the sky to the ground.

Jacob watched the angels in his dream. "Who are they? Where did they come from? Why are they here?" he wondered.

Then he heard a voice saying, "I am the God of Abraham, your grandfather, and the God of Isaac, your father. I know it's hard for you to leave your home and family. Don't worry. I'll protect you. I want you to know that this land will be yours someday and that it will be the land of your children. You will have many children. You will have a big family and they will live in every part of this land – in the mountains, in the valleys, and near the sea. I am your God. I will be with you and watch you wherever you go. I will bring you back to this land, the land of Canaan. I will not leave you."

Jacob woke up. He looked around. It was very quiet. It was morning and he was still lying on the ground. He wondered, "Where am I? Where is the ladder and where are the angels?" Then he knew that it was a dream. He remembered that a voice had spoken to him. He thought, "God is in this place and I didn't know it. This place is very special."

Jacob got ready to continue on his trip. As he was leaving he noticed the stone that he had used as a pillow. "See," he said as he picked up the stone. "You helped me. Even though you are a hard stone, you were a comfortable pillow."

Then he put the stone back in its place and poured oil on it. "God is in this place," he said. "From now on this place will be called Beth El, the House of God. The stone with oil on it will show that this is a special place."

Then Jacob took all of his things and continued on his way. He felt good.

Questions on the Theme
1. What were Jacob's feelings when he left his home?
2. What did Jacob think about his dream after he woke up? Did he like it? (5 and 6-year-olds)
3. What did Jacob do to show that the place where he had his dream was a special place?

In Haran

Jacob continued on his way. He thought, "I've gone a long way. I must be getting closer to Haran."

Suddenly, he noticed a group of sheep and goats in the distance. He came closer and closer to them and saw shepherds, too. They were standing near a well. The shepherds noticed him.

Jacob called, "Where are you from?"

"We're from Haran," was their answer.

Then Jacob asked, "Do you know Laban?"

"Yes, of course," said the shepherds.

"How is he and how is his family?" asked Jacob.

"They are all well. Oh look, here comes his daughter Rachel now. She's bringing her father's sheep to the well."

As Jacob turned to look, he saw a young woman coming closer with her goats and sheep. She was pretty. He liked the way she looked.

He turned to the shepherds and asked, "Why do you just stand here near the well? Give your sheep water."

"We can't," said the shepherds. "There's a big stone over the well. When all of the shepherds come here with their flocks, we'll roll the stone from the well together. Then when we're finished getting water, we'll roll it back together."

Jacob noticed that Rachel stood near the well with her flock. He walked to the well. He pushed and shoved and pushed and shoved the stone until at last it rolled away from the well. "Here," he said as he turned to Rachel, "let me help you give water to your flock."

"Oh," said Rachel in surprise. She wondered, "Who is this stranger who is helping me?"

Jacob could see that Rachel was curious about him. "Rachel, I am not a stranger. I am your cousin. I am Jacob, the son of Isaac and Rebecca, your father's sister. I have come here from the faraway land of Canaan."

"Really?" shouted Rachel in surprise. "I must go and tell my father." Then she turned and quickly ran home with Jacob following behind her.

"Father, father," she called as she reached her house. Someone came to us from the land of Canaan."

Laban was surprised. "Who is it?"

"It's Jacob, the son of Isaac and Rebecca. He helped me give water to the sheep."

"We must invite him into our home right away," called Laban as he ran out to meet Jacob.

When they saw each other, Laban and Jacob hugged and kissed. "Come into my house and be my guest," said Laban smiling. "Thank you so much, Uncle," said Jacob. "It's good to be here after such a long and tiring trip."

Questions on the Story

1. Were Jacob and Rachel happy to see each other? Why?
2. Do you think it's easy or difficult to take care of sheep and goats? What needs to be done?
3. Why do you think there was a big stone on the well? (5 and 6-year-olds)

THEMES IN THE STORY

Jacob Leaves His Home

Jacob prepared for his difficult journey to Haran in a big hurry. He may not have had time to make all the usual preparations.

Bringing the Theme Closer

- Provide the children with some background information on travel in biblical times. Explain that travel in those days was very complicated and required a great deal of preparation and planning. When Jacob traveled to his mother's family home in Paddan-Aram, he had to travel a great distance over a dry and difficult terrain. Help the children to understand the process involved by explaining that Jacob had to travel on foot or on a donkey. When he wanted to rest, he had to set up camp and sleep on the ground. Jacob had to take his own food along. If he needed water, he had to find a stream or a well.

Jacob Has a Dream

Jacob's dreams were very important to him. He felt that they were meaningful and that he could learn from them.

Bringing the Theme Closer
- Encourage children to discuss the sequence of events in Jacob's dream by asking: What was the first thing that Jacob did to get ready to sleep? Then what did he do? What did Jacob dream about? What happened to Jacob in his dream?
- Did you ever have a dream? What happened in your dream? How did it feel when you woke up?

Jacob Meets Rachel at the Well

This story emphasizes the importance of wells and the conservation of water in the times of the Patriarchs. The well was the central focus of the community – a place to water the animals, to get water for home, and a place for cooperation and social interaction.

Bringing the Theme Closer
- Discuss why water is so important for plants, animals, and human beings. Some children may be aware, through T.V., of the effect of a lack of water. Explain the words "conservation" and "drought." Brainstorm with the children ways they can conserve water usage.
- Encourage the children to review Jacob's relationships – Jacob and Rebecca, Jacob and Esau, Jacob and Isaac. How was each person affected by the behavior of the other? How is Jacob related to Rebecca, to Esau, to Isaac, to Rachel? What are the good aspects of each relationship? What are aspects of each relationship that are not so good?

Jacob Has Faith That God Will Help Him

Jacob does not know what awaits him, but he goes on his journey with confidence and hope strengthened by his faith in God.

Bringing the Theme Closer
- Talk with the children about Jacob's attitudes toward his future and toward God. Then ask: Did you ever go to a place where you haven't been before? What was it like? What did you do? Were you alone? Who was with you?

CREATIVE FOLLOW UP

Retelling the Story

Goals

To encourage children to think about the story in terms of colors.
To stimulate the children's imagination.
To reinforce the names of colors.

FINGER PAINTING (3 AND 4-YEAR-OLDS)

Description of Project

Children describe through finger paints colors which they think are very important in the story (e.g., green grass, blue sky, etc.).

Materials

finger paints (store bought, made with pudding, or made with the recipe below)

Procedure

1. Ask children which colors are important to this story (the color of the grass, of the sky, of the animals, etc.).
2. Provide the ingredients for making finger paints and prepare as described below (or use pudding or the ready-made variety).
3. Encourage the children to use the color or colors they think might have been in the story.
4. After the paintings have dried, review key points of the story.
5. Encourage children to show their pictures to the rest of the group and to describe them and their colors.

Finger Paints

Ingredients

    1 cup laundry starch
    1 cup cold water
    3 cups soap flakes

Method

    1. Mix the starch, water, and soap flakes together.
    2. Add tempera paints for color.

STRING PAINTING (5 and 6-year-olds)

Description of Activity

Children describe the colors which they think are very important in the story.

Materials

    drawing paper
    small, shallow bowls
    6 pieces of string, each about 9" long
    tempera paint in blue, green, brown

Procedure

1. Ask children which colors are important to the story (e.g., the color of the grass, sky, animals, etc.).
2. On a table, place bowls of tempera paint (blue, green brown). Put two pieces of string in each bowl.
3. Show children how to dip a string into the paint and move it across a piece of drawing paper.
4. Encourage the children to use the color or colors they think might have been in the story.
5. After the paintings have dried, review key points of the story.
6. Invite children to show their pictures to the rest of the group and to describe them and the colors they used.

TABLE TOP FLANNEL BOARD (3 TO 6-YEAR-OLDS)

Goals

To help the child to integrate the sequence of events.
To develop an understanding of the personalities of the characters.
To help children understand how others feel when they move to a new place.

Description of Activity

Children communicate with their peers through the use of a flannel board.

Materials

bottom of a square cardboard carton (or piece of masonite)
scissors or X-acto knife
light colored flannel
stapler
pellon
felt markers

Procedure

1. Help children make a flannel board. Begin by cutting a rectangular shape of cardboard.
2. Divide the cardboard into four equal sections by scoring in three places as shown in the diagram :

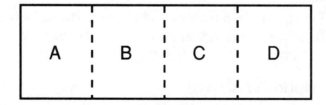

3. Fold section A under section D as shown in the diagram below:

4. Cover one exposed area with flannel and staple to corners as shown in the diagram below:

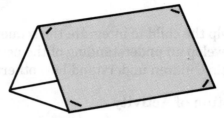

5. Draw stick figures and stones, camels, sheep, and a well onto pieces of pellon with felt marker.
6. Encourage children to suggest characters and objects from the story for the teacher to draw on additional pieces of pellon.
7. The teacher and the children use the flannel board to retell the story.
8. Keep the flannel board and its accessories in the Bible corner for use by the children during the free play time.

Science

WATER CONSERVATION (3 AND 4-YEAR-OLDS)

Goals

To help children understand the importance of water.
To help children understand how water supplies were protected in biblical times.

Description of Activity

Children learn about water conservation through a science activity.

Materials

2 glass bowls, one with a cover
water
red felt marker

Procedure

1. Discuss the importance of water and why it is necessary to protect a water supply.
2. Discuss some of the uses of water.

3. Fill two bowls about ¾ full with water. Leave one bowl uncovered. Cover the second bowl.
4. Put the bowls on a window sill.
5. Every other day, look at the bowls with the children. With a felt marker, indicate the water level on the outside of each bowl.
6. Discuss how the cover protects the water.

WATER EVAPORATION (5 AND 6-YEAR-OLDS)

Goals

To help children understand the importance of water.
To help children begin to understand that water evaporates in a hot climate.

Description of Activity

Children learn about evaporation by doing a science experiment.

Materials

Pyrex saucepan
2 cups water
stove or hot plate
pot holder
red felt marker

Procedure

1. Discuss with a small group of 4-5 children the importance of water and the uses of water.
2. Discuss the special importance of water in the hot summer.
3. Fill the saucepan with the 2 cups of water and mark the level on the outside of the bowl with a red felt marker.
4. Put the saucepan on the stove or hot plate on a very low temperature to simulate the heat in the desert. (Discuss the rules when standing near a stove or hot plate – handle of pot moved to side, don't stand too close, etc.)
5. After 15 minutes, look at the water level in the pot and mark it with a felt marker.
6. Explain that the heat of the stove makes the water evaporate, just as it evaporates in the heat of the desert. It is for this reason that water is very precious in a desert climate.

Game Time

Goals

To identify the important elements of the story.
To help the children classify objects from the story.

WHAT'S MISSING? (3 AND 4-YEAR-OLDS)

Description of Activity

Children review the important elements of the story.

Materials

5 ½" x 8" pieces of posterboard (or index cards)
8 ½" x 11" pieces of posterboard
felt markers

Procedure

1. Summarize the story with the children.
2. Ask children to identify the important elements of the story. List these on an experience chart.
3. On the left half of the easel, sketch pictures, each of which lacks one important item (e.g., a tent with one side missing, a camel with the hump missing, a tree with the trunk missing, a sheep with one leg missing, a rider in a caravan without a donkey under him/her, a person bending over a well with nothing attached to the end of the rope he/she is holding).
4. The teacher then copies the picture onto the left half of an 8 ½" x 11" piece of posterboard as shown in the diagram below:

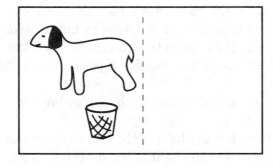

5. After a series of pictures and accompanying cards have been created, invite the children to match the cards with the pictures.
6. Children can play this game individually, in pairs, and in small groups.

WHAT'S MISSING? (5 AND 6-YEAR-OLDS)

Description of Activity
Children recreate important elements of the story.

Materials
5 ½" x 8" pieces of posterboard (or index cards)
8 ½" x 11" pieces of posterboard
felt markers

Procedure
1. The children sit in a semi-circle on the floor or on chairs, facing the teacher.
2. Summarize the story with the children.
3. Begin telling the story, leaving out certain important elements.
4. A child who realizes that something has been omitted stands up. The teacher calls on that child to explain to the others the details of the missing part of the story.
5. Continue in this way until the story has been finished.

TAKING THE STORY HOME

1. Send home a note encouraging parents to allow their child to stay up one evening to look at the night sky as Jacob had. Remind parents to check the weather report so that they can choose a clear, starry night. Ask parents to point out the moon and clusters of stars, emphasizing that these were created by God. Have them talk with their child about what they are seeing and what Jacob saw.
2. Suggest that parents take their child to a grassy area where they should make a circle on the grass about a yard in diameter with a plastic hoop or a rope. The parent identifies one item in the circle that God made. The child investigates and identifies a second item that God made. Parent and child take turns until there seem to be no more items to name. Then, using a

magnifying glass, examine the area again. Are there things that can be seen that could not be seen with the naked eye? Conclude the activity by discussing the things that Jacob saw that were made by God.

3. Send home a list of story starters for children to complete. Examples follow:
   - When Jacob slept outside he . . .
   - When Jacob was hungry on his trip he . . .
   - Jacob knew which way to go because . . .

CHAPTER 6

Jacob Raises a Family

BEFORE TELLING THE STORY

1. Review with the children pertinent aspects of Jacob's life (Jacob's personality – quiet, subdued; the reason that Jacob left his home and family; Jacob as a shepherd – refer back to Jacob's father, Isaac, and to his grandfather, Abraham, who were shepherds also).
2. Consider what a shepherd does, what his or her responsibilities are, and how such a person spends his/her long hours in the field.

TELLING THE STORY

At Laban's House

Jacob lived in Laban's house. He ate and slept and helped with the work there. Everyone liked him. He especially liked Rachel. "She is so nice and so pretty," he thought to himself. "I really love her and I think she loves me, too." His love for her grew more and more each day.

One day Jacob said to Laban, "Since I have been living in your house, I have been meeting Rachel every day. I love her very much. I want to marry her. Please let me marry her."

Laban listened. He thought for a while. Then he said, "I am very happy that my sister's son wants to marry my daughter. But first you must work for me for seven years. Then you can marry her."

Jacob was pleased. "Good," he said. "I will do it." And that was what he did.

When Jacob woke up each day, he was content. He worked hard taking care of Laban's flock. He worked day after day, week after week, month after month, and year after year. Laban was pleased with Jacob's work. Jacob counted the passing years. They seemed to pass quickly: one, two, three, four, five, six, seven.

At last Jacob said to Laban, "I've worked for you for seven years. Now I will marry Rachel as we agreed."

"You are right," said Laban. "But first you will marry Rachel's older sister Leah. Here in this place the older daughter must be married before the younger one. If you promise to work for me for another seven years you may marry Rachel."

Jacob was disappointed and upset. He had worked hard for Laban so he could marry Rachel. Now he needed to work another seven years. Yet, he loved Rachel so much that he agreed to Laban's plan. He married Leah. And then he married Rachel. In those days men often had more than one wife.

Questions on the Story

1. How was Jacob welcomed into Laban's family?
2. What is the hardest work you ever did? Did you receive anything special for doing the work?

Jacob's Children

Jacob lived with his two wives. Leah gave birth to a son and then another son and then another son. She had six sons and one daughter. They brought her much happiness.

Rachel had no children. When she saw how much Jacob loved Leah's children, she felt terrible that she had none. Each day when Jacob came home from work, he saw that Rachel's eyes were red. She had been crying.

"Why do you cry, Rachel?" he asked as he hugged her.

"I'm sad because I don't have children. I want to take care of them and to watch them grow," she said.

"Don't worry Rachel, you have me to be with and I love you very much." But Rachel still felt sad.

One morning when Rachel awoke, she had an unusual feeling inside of her. She knew she was pregnant. She could hardly wait to tell Jacob. When he came home from work, she ran to him with a smile on her face.

"Jacob, a wonderful thing has happened! In a few months I am going to have a baby!" Her eyes sparkled with excitement. Jacob was very pleased to hear the wonderful news! Rachel could hardly wait for the months to pass. They seemed to pass slowly.

At last, the day came when Rachel gave birth to a beautiful baby boy. They called him Joseph. There was great joy in Jacob's family.

Jacob now had a big family: eleven sons and one daughter. The sons were Reuben, Simeon, Levi, Judah, Issachar, Zebulon, Dan, Naphtali, Gad, Asher, and Joseph. His daughter was named Dina. Jacob, Leah, and Rachel loved their children and took good care of them.

Questions on the Story
1. Why was Rachel sad at first when she thought she might not have children?
2. What did Rachel and Jacob name their son?
3. Do you know anyone named Jacob, Leah, Rachel, Dan, or Dina?

THEMES IN THE STORY

Jacob's Position in Laban's Household

Jacob had responsibilities as Laban's shepherd. Young children also have responsibilities, both at home and in the classroom. A young child can be helped to understand that his/her job at school is important to a smooth running classroom, and that other children depend on him/her to do whatever job is assigned.

Bringing the Theme Closer
- Discuss how Jacob became part of Laban's family. Ask: How do you make a guest feel part of your family? How do you help a new child in school? Read *Will I Have a Friend?* by Miriam Cohen. Use this book as the basis for the discussion.
- What did Jacob think about when he was out with the sheep?
- How do you think Jacob took care of the sheep? How do you take care of a pet dog or cat?
- What did Jacob think about life in Laban's house?

- What is your job in the class? What are you responsible for? What do you think would happen if you didn't do your job?

Promises and Goals

This episode focuses on the promises which Jacob and Laban made to each other. Jacob promised to work for seven more years and Laban promised to allow Jacob to marry Rachel.

Bringing the Theme Closer

- Have you ever been to a wedding? What does the bride wear? What do you think is special about a wedding?
- What did Jacob think about working for another seven years in order to marry Rachel?
- What can you say when someone promises you something, but doesn't keep his promise?
- How do you think Jacob felt when he knew that each day that he worked, he was getting closer to marrying Rachel?
- What are some ways that Jacob could count or mark the days until he would marry Rachel? What are some ways that you count or mark the days until you do something special (birthday, go on a trip, etc.)? Shabbat is a special day that comes every week. What are ways that we count, mark, or prepare for Shabbat?

Rachel Wishes She Had Children

Sarah wished that she had children. Rebecca wished that she had children. And now Rachel wished that she would have children. Young children are somewhat aware of the changes in a pregnant woman and the changes that an expected baby brings to a family.

Bringing the Theme Closer

- Ask: Do you know anyone who is pregnant? How can you tell?
- On the bulletin board, place pictures of babies, as well as pictures of mother, father, and siblings holding a baby.

CREATIVE FOLLOW UP

Retelling the Story

Goals

To reinforce information acquired during the telling of the story.
To help the children sequence the events of the story.

ROLE PLAY (3 AND 4-YEAR-OLDS)

Description of Project

Children learn about the perspective of others through role play.

Materials

a large box
bathrobes
scarves
jewelry
carpet squares
sandals
a sheet

Procedure

1. Create a prop box with the materials listed above.
2. The teacher encourages the children to play the roles of Jacob, Rachel, and Leah. As they pretend to be these characters, they use materials from the prop box in ways that seem appropriate to them.
3. Children then volunteer to assume roles of specific story characters and narrate the story.
4. Place the sheet over a table or desk to simulate a tent.
5. Children continue to role play in this organized fashion, as well as on their own during the free activity period.
6. Incorporate the prop box into the Bible corner.

ROLE PLAY (5 AND 6-YEAR-OLDS)

Description of Activity

Children learn about the perspective of others through role play.

Materials

a large box
bathrobes
scarves
jewelry
carpet squares
sandals
a sheet

Procedure

1. Create a prop box with the materials listed above.
2. The teacher encourages the children to play the roles of Jacob, Rachel, and Leah. As they pretend to be these characters, they use materials from the prop box in ways that seem appropriate to them.
3. Children then volunteer to assume roles of specific story characters and narrate the story.
4. Place the sheet over a table or desk to simulate a tent.
5. Children continue to role play in this organized fashion, as well as on their own during the free activity period.
6. Incorporate the prop box into the Bible corner.
7. Ask children to bring materials from home to add to the prop box.
8. Children role play specific parts of the story for each other and for other classes.

Game Time

Goals

To help the children learn classification.
To provide labels for the children.

MATCHING ADULT AND BABY ANIMALS (3 AND 4-YEAR-OLDS)

Description of Activity

Children match adult animals with their babies and learn the names of the animals.

Materials

pictures of baby animals (calf, colt, kid, lamb, puppy, kitten, etc.)
pictures of adult animals (cow, horse, goat, dog, cat, sheep, etc.)

construction paper
white glue

Procedure
1. Find pictures of animals mentioned in the story, as well as others with which the children are familiar.
2. Mount and secure each picture on a piece of construction paper with white glue.
3. Introduce the pictures to children in small groups. Encourage children to use the pictures in pairs or in small groups.
4. Help the children to match pairs (baby and adult) and identify them.

MATCHING ADULT AND BABY ANIMALS (5 AND 6-YEAR-OLDS)

Description of Activity
Children match adult animals with their babies, learn the names of the animals, and learn to recognize the written names of each species.

Materials
pictures of baby animals (calf, colt, kid, lamb, puppy, kitten, etc.)
pictures of adult animals (cow, horse, goat, dog, cat, sheep, etc.)
construction paper
white glue
felt markers
construction paper
scissors

Procedure
1. Find pictures of animals mentioned in the story, as well as others with which the children are familiar.
2. Mount and secure each picture on a piece of construction paper with white glue.
3. Introduce the pictures to children in small groups. Encourage children to use the pictures in pairs or in small groups.
4. Help the children to match pairs (baby and adult) and identify them.
5. Cut construction paper into 5 ½" x 8" pieces.
6. Write the name of an adult animal and its baby on each piece of cut construction paper.

7. Introduce the three sets of cards to children in pairs or in small groups. Encourage the groups to match pictures of adults with babies and to identify the written names of each species.

Story Time

Goals

To help the children understand people's feelings in different situations.
To help the children understand how to manage feelings.

READ AND DISCUSS (3 AND 4-YEAR-OLDS)

Description of Activity

Teacher reads books about feelings as a springboard for discussing the story.

Materials

Feelings by Terry Berger
I Have Feelings by Terry Berger
Will I Have a Friend? by Miriam Cohen

Procedure

1. Read one or more of the books listed above.
2. Discuss the feelings that are described in the book.
3. Ask the children when they have experienced the feelings described in the book(s).
4. Compare these feelings (e.g., fear, anger, worry about friendship) with Jacob's feelings in the story.

READ AND DISCUSS (5 AND 6-YEAR-OLDS)

Description of Activity

Teacher reads books about feelings as a springboard for discussing the story.

Materials

Sometimes I'm Afraid by Jane Watson, Robert Switzer, J. Cotter Hirschberg
Sometimes I Get Angry by Jane Watson, Robert Switzer, J. Cotter Hirschberg
It's Scary Sometimes by Marcella Bacigalupi, et al

Procedure

1. Read one or more of the books listed above.
2. Discuss the feelings that are described in the book.
3. Ask the children when they have experienced the feelings described in the book(s).
4. Compare these feelings (e.g., fear, anger, worry about friendship) with Jacob's feelings in the story.

TAKING THE STORY HOME

1. Suggest that parents to review the story and then encourage their child to use the materials in their Bible Box for dramatic play with siblings and friends.
2. Suggest that parents make a classification game, *What Fits?* for their child. Send home a synopsis of the story and the following list of materials and instructions:

Materials

> a magazine with large, colorful pictures
> child-size pictures
> glue
> a sheet of construction paper 11" x 17"
> 2 #10 envelopes
> felt marker

To Make the Board:

> Write the word "Fits" on one envelope and the words "Doesn't Fit" on the other. Glue the two envelopes side-by-side on the construction paper.

To Play:

> Encourage your child to look through the magazine for pictures showing objects which might have been in the Bible story, and for pictures which were probably not in the Bible story. The child may cut or rip out the pictures and place them in the appropriate envelope. As this is being done, involve your child in conversation about the reasons for the choices.

3. Send home a list of story starters for the children to complete. Examples follow:
   - Jacob worked hard for seven years because he wanted to . . .
   - Rachel was sad because . . .
   - Rachel was happy when she was pregnant because . . .
   - Jacob and his wives were happy because . . .

CHAPTER 7

Jacob Moves Back to Canaan

BEFORE TELLING THE STORY

1. Review with the children the sequence of events that brought Jacob to Haran.
2. Write each of the following headings on an experience chart: Things That Shepherds Do, Things That Husbands Do, Things That Fathers Do. Encourage the children's involvement in completing the charts. Discuss which of these things Jacob might have done in his roles as shepherd, husband, and father.

TELLING THE STORY

Back to Canaan

One evening Jacob called his wives and children together. He said to them, "This place where we live now is not our land. Our land is Canaan. Twenty years ago I ran away from Canaan and I came to live here in Haran with Laban. I always knew, though, that I would go back to my land in Canaan. Even though my brother Esau is angry with me, I must go back to the land of Canaan to live. Esau and I are brothers. We will find a way to be friends and to live peacefully."

The next day Jacob said to Laban, "I've lived in your house for many years and now I have a big family. I've worked hard for you while I was here. Are you satisfied with my work?"

"Yes," said Laban. "Your hard work has made me rich. Today I have many goats and lambs and donkeys and camels and cows and bulls. But why must you leave?"

"I need to go back to live in the land of Canaan. God promised it to my father, Isaac, and to my grandfather, Abraham. But before I leave I want to take some of your animals. I worked hard for many years raising them. I think some of them should be mine."

For a few moments Laban was silent. Then he said, "You can take what you deserve. If it is important for you to go back to Canaan, take your family and go. I will miss you all."

Jacob had a great deal to do to get ready for the trip. He called his family together and said, "We will soon leave Haran. We have a long trip to prepare for. Everyone must help us get ready. Everyone will have a job. Laban and I will decide which animals I will take."

Food for the trip was prepared and loaded onto donkeys and camels. Jacob and his helpers gathered the flock for the trip. They gave the animals water. At last, the time came to leave.

Questions on the Story

1. Why did Jacob have to go back to Canaan?
2. How do you think Leah and Rachel felt about going to a new home?
3. What things do you think they took along for their journey?
4. Do you know any other people from Bible stories who left their home?

The Journey

Very early in the morning before the sun rose, the caravan left for the land of Canaan. Jacob was in the lead on a camel. Rebecca and Leah and the children rode on camels, too. The animals and the shepherds followed behind. The caravan traveled for many days, passing through valleys and over hills.

"Meh, meh," said the sheep.

"Kalump, kalump," went the camels' feet.

"Jingle, jingle," went the bells on the camels.

They traveled on and on day after day, but they always stopped at night to rest.

One evening they came to a stream. Jacob stopped and thought for a moment. Then he turned to his family and said, "After we cross the stream we will be very close to where Esau is. I think he knows that we are here, but we don't know what he plans to do. In the meantime, let's set up camp near this stream."

The family spread blankets on the ground and sat down to eat. When they finished eating, they lay down on the blankets and rested. It was quiet. The moon was shining.

Jacob called several of his men together. He said to them, "Tomorrow morning, find Esau. Tell him I've been living with Laban until now. I have many animals and many people in my household. Now that I am back in Canaan, I hope Esau and I can be friends."

When Jacob's men returned, they looked tired and worried.

"What happened?" Jacob asked. "Did you meet Esau?"

"Yes. He was getting ready to meet you and he has four hundred men with him."

Jacob was afraid. He thought a moment. "We'll have to be ready to defend ourselves just in case Esau attacks us."

So Jacob divided all of his people into two groups. One group went in one direction and the other went the other way. If Esau attacked one group, the other would be saved.

But Jacob was still worried. He couldn't sleep that night. He kept wondering how he could make Esau feel better. He prayed to God, "God of Abraham, my grandfather, and God of Isaac, my father, you said I must return to my land and you promised to help me. Save us now if Esau attacks us." Then Jacob fell into a deep sleep.

Questions on the Story

1. Why do you think Jacob was afraid that Esau might attack the caravan?
2. Why did Jacob send several of his men ahead to find Esau?
3. What do you think about Jacob's plan to send one half of his people in one direction and the other half in the other direction?
4. What is a caravan? What is its purpose? When is it needed? (5 and 6-year-olds)

The Gifts

In the morning, Jacob woke up before the others. He thought, "Esau loves presents. I think that if he sees a lot of presents, he will truly believe that I want to live in peace."

Then he woke the shepherds up and called to them. "Quickly! Get up and take all these presents to Esau – goats, lambs, cows, bulls, camels, and donkeys."

The shepherds went quickly to search for Esau. When they found him, they showed him the goats and lambs. Esau asked, "Who are you and whose animals are these?"

"We are Jacob's shepherds," they answered. "He has sent you these animals as gifts. He and his family will be here in a few days." Esau was pleased with the gifts.

After a while, cows and bulls were brought to Esau. "Who are you and whose animals are these?" he asked.

"We also are Jacob's shepherds. He sends still more animals to you as gifts. He wants you to forgive him." Esau smiled.

Then a group of camels and donkeys arrived. "Jacob sends you even more gifts," said the shepherds. "He wants you to forgive him."

Esau looked at everything and said, "Go back and tell Jacob that I'm ready to meet him and his family."

Meanwhile, Jacob and his people waited for the shepherds to return.

God spoke to Jacob and said, "Your name is Jacob, but from now on you will be called Israel." And from that time on he was sometimes called Jacob and sometimes he was called Israel.

Questions on the Story
1. What do you think will happen when Jacob and Esau meet each other again?
2. What did Jacob do to show Esau that he wanted to be on good terms with his brother again?
3. Did Esau decide to make up with Jacob?
4. Do you think God had a special reason for giving Jacob another name?

The Brothers Meet Again

Jacob thought he saw something moving in the distance. Soon he could see many, many people. Then he saw that it was Esau and his men. Jacob called to his people, "Look, it's Esau and his men. Let's welcome them nicely."

Jacob ran to meet Esau. When Esau saw Jacob running to him, he ran, too. They met and hugged and kissed. Then they cried. They looked into each other's eyes.

"Oh, how long I have waited for this moment!" said Jacob.

"I'm so happy to see you, too," said Esau with a big grin. "Now we can live together peacefully as brothers."

Esau noticed Jacob's caravan of women, children, shepherds, and animals. "Who are all these?"

"This is my family. God blessed me with a large family," said Jacob proudly.

Then Esau asked, "Why did you send me so many animals?"

"They are presents from me," answered Jacob. "I have enough. I want you to have them because you forgave me."

The brothers hugged each other again and promised to live together in peace. When they finished talking together, Esau went back to his home and Jacob continued on with his caravan. He was now back in the land of Canaan.

At last, Jacob came to Shechem. He decided to stay there with his big family. And what a wonderful surprise they had when Rachel gave birth to a second son. They named him Benjamin.

Then God said to Israel, "You have a very large family with many children. You will have many, many grandchildren, and you will live with your family in the land which I gave to Abraham, to Isaac, and now to you." And that was what happened. Jacob had twelve sons: Reuben, Simeon, Levi, Judah, Issachar, Zebulon, Joseph, Benjamin, Dan, Naphtali, Gad, Asher, and a daughter Dina. Jacob was very proud of his big family, and he loved them very much.

It was a very sad time for Jacob when Rachel died. As his children grew bigger and bigger, he thought about Rachel many times and he wished she could be with him.

Questions on the Story

1. What did Jacob and Esau do when they met?
2. Were Jacob and Esau happy that they made up? Why?
3. What did Rachel and Jacob call their new baby?
4. How did Jacob feel when Rachel died?
5. What are the names of some of Jacob's children?

THEMES IN THE STORY

Jacob and His Family Return to Canaan

Jacob wanted to return to his birthplace, Canaan. For everyone, except Jacob, this was a move to an unfamiliar country. Young children can identify with a move to a new location, with making new friends and settling in.

Bringing the Theme Closer

- How do you think Laban felt when Jacob said he wanted to leave and take his family to Canaan?
- Have you ever moved to a different house? Have you ever moved to a different city? What was it like to move?
- How do you think Jacob and his family prepared for their trip? How do you get ready for a trip? What do you pack?
- What do you think Leah and Rachel talked about as they were leaving their father's house? (5 and 6-year-olds)

Jacob Meets Esau

Children can relate to the idea of people meeting after many years apart. They are also familiar with the concept of "making up" after a disagreement.

Bringing the Theme Closer

- What did Jacob think would happen when he met Esau? What did Esau think would happen?
- Have you ever camped out? How and what did you eat? What do you have to take along when you prepare to go camping?
- What do you think about Jacob sending gifts to Esau?
- Would you rather have one big present or several smaller presents?

- Why do you think Jacob was worried about meeting Esau again? Was it a good idea to be worried?
- Have you ever been angry with someone or has someone been angry with you? How did you "make up"?
- What did Jacob think when he saw Esau again?
- What did Esau think when he saw Jacob again?
- How could Jacob and Esau have recognized each other after so many years?
- What do you think Jacob and Esau will say to each other the next time they meet?

CREATIVE FOLLOW-UP

Retelling the Story

Goals

To reinforce information acquired during the telling of the story.
To help the children sequence the events of the story.

PAPER BAG HAND PUPPETS (3 AND 4-YEAR-OLDS)

Description of Activity

Children communicate with their peers through the use of puppets.

Materials

paper lunch bags
scraps of colored paper
yarn
cotton balls
white glue
scissors
buttons

Procedure

1. Gather 3 or 4 children together and review the story.
2. Discuss the characters and animals in the story.
3. Show the children the materials for making puppets. Discuss ways to make a hand puppet.

4. Provide the materials at easy access and encourage each child to create several of the characters or animals in the story as puppets (see diagram below):

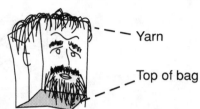

5. Put your hand in a paper lunch bag to demonstrate how to use the puppet. Encourage the children to do the same.
6. Sit with the children and discuss with them their characters and animals.
7. The children use the puppets to create skits for the small group.
8. At a later time, children can create skits with their puppets for the entire class.
9. Let the children take their puppets home (see Taking the Story Home below).

PAPER BAG PEOPLE PUPPETS (5 AND 6-YEAR-OLDS)

Description of Activity
Children create puppets and dramatize the story.

Materials
large paper grocery bags, one for each child
yarn
paint
cotton balls
white glue
scissors
fabric

Procedure
1. Gather 3 to 6 children together and review the story.
2. Discuss the characters and animals in the story.

3. Provide the materials at easy access. Show the materials to the children and ask for ideas for decorating the puppets.
4. Encourage each child to begin creating a puppet (see diagram below):

5. Help each child to cut armholes in their bag. Also help each to cut holes for eyes.
6. Sit with the children and discuss with them their characters and animals.
7. The children use the puppets to dramatize the characters for their small group.
8. At a later time children perform with their puppets for the entire class.
9. Let the children take their puppets home (see Taking the Story Home below).

Note: Shy children generally feel more protected behind this kind of puppet than any other type. Nonetheless, do not force a child to use this type of puppet if he or she doesn't like his/her head covered.

Rhythms

Goals

To encourage recall of story.
To encourage the children to take turns.

WE ARE JACOB'S FAMILY (3 AND 4-YEAR-OLDS)

Description of Activity

Children use rhythms to express their interpretation of leaving for Canaan.

Materials

chairs and carpet squares or a small carpet

Procedure

1. The children sit in a circle.
2. Establish a rhythm by tapping your knees (twice) and clapping your hands (twice) and encourage the children to imitate you.
3. As they do so, say, "We are Jacob's family. We are going to Canaan. We will take water." (This helps the children to begin the sequence of the game.) The first child says, "We are Jacob's family. We are going to Canaan. We will take _____." These sentences are repeated by the group and each subsequent child completes the sentence in turn.

WE ARE JACOB'S FAMILY (5 AND 6-YEAR-OLDS)

Description of Activity

Children use rhythms to express their interpretations of leaving for Canaan.

Materials

chairs and carpet squares or a small carpet

Procedure

1. The children sit in a circle.
2. Establish a rhythm by tapping your knees (twice) and clapping your hands (twice) and encourage the children to imitate you.
3. Say, "We are Jacob's family. We are going to Canaan. We will take water." The first child repeats these sentences and adds another item to be taken. Each subsequent child repeats the initial sentence and the items to be taken and adds something new.

Game Time

LOTTO (3 AND 4-YEAR-OLDS)

Goals

To facilitate the development of classification skills.
To reinforce the events of the story.

Materials

8 sheets of construction paper 8 ½" x 11"
scissors
white glue
10 pictures (see page 99)
24 peanuts or disks

Procedure

1. Make the lotto board and the game cards according to the directions below.
2. Play the game according to the instructions below.

To make the lotto board:

1. Photocopy each of the 10 pictures 4 times to make a total of 48 pictures.
2. Glue the pictures to four pieces of construction paper, six to a sheet (see diagram below).

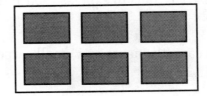

To make game cards:

1. Cut up each of the other 4 sheets of construction paper into 6 parts so that there are 24 pieces of paper.
2. Cut up each of the remaining 24 pictures to make cards.

Instructions for play:

1. Each of 3 players will need a lotto board and a pile of peanuts or disks.
2. Place the small picture cards face down on the table. One player picks a card from the top of the pile and matches it with the identical one on the lotto board. Each player then places a peanut on the same picture on his/her lotto board.
3. The card is then placed at the bottom of the pile and the next player draws another card from the top of the pile.

4. Continue in this manner until everyone has a marker on each of the spaces on his/her lotto board.

CONCENTRATION (5 AND 6-YEAR-OLDS)

Goals

To help children review objects and animals in the story.
To facilitate the development of memory skills.

Description of Activity

Children review objects and animals in the story through a game.

Materials

package of 5" x 8" index cards, unlined
scissors
glue
box
pictures in duplicate of a goat, a lamb, camel, sack, donkey, mule, caravan, trees, landscape, tent (many of these can be found in the section at the back of this book)

Procedure

1. Prior to class, glue both pictures of each object or animal to an index card. Keep the pack of pictures in a box.
2. Follow the instructions for play below.

Instructions for Play:

1. Place all the cards face down and spread out on a table top.
2. One child turns over any 2 cards. If the cards are the same, the child takes the cards and gets another turn. If the cards do not match, another child takes a turn.
3. Ask each child to identify and describe the pictures on the cards he/she turns over.

TAKING THE STORY HOME

1. Each child brings his/her puppets home. Send parents a list of puppet activities appropriate for the home. Suggest that they cover a table with a

sheet or tablecloth to make a stage, then act out the following scenes with the puppets:

a. Jacob telling his family that he wants to go back to Canaan and the reactions of family members to this announcement.

b. Jacob and his family and animals on their journey. What were the things the people said and the sounds the animals made?

c. Jacob talking with the shepherds about the gifts he would send to Esau. What did the shepherds say were good gifts?

d. Esau looking at the gifts Jacob sent him. What did Esau say to the shepherds when he received them?

e. Jacob and Esau meeting with each other for the first time after so many years. What did they say to each other?

2. Send home a description of the game *We Are Jacob's Family*. Encourage families to play it according to the procedure appropriate for their child's age group (see above).

3. Send home a list of story starters for the children to complete. Examples follow:

   * Jacob wanted to go back to Canaan because . . .
   * When Jacob and his family traveled to Canaan, they took with them . . .
   * After traveling for a while, Jacob and his family stopped to rest. They put blankets on the ground and . . .
   * Before Jacob met Esau, he sent Esau some . . .
   * When Jacob and Esau saw each other, they . . .

CHAPTER 8

Joseph

BEFORE TELLING THE STORY

1. Review with the children aspects of Jacob's life which are relevant to this story: Jacob's relationship with his parents and with his brother Esau, Jacob's marriage to Rachel and Leah, the birth of Jacob's children.
2. Sibling rivalry and family relationships are major themes in this story. Read one or more of the following books which depict family relationships: *What the Moon Brought* by Sadie Rose Weilerstein (5 and 6-year-olds), *Where's My Truck?* by Anne Sibley O'Brien (3-year-olds), *Let Me Tell You About My Baby* by Roslyn Banish (3 to 6-year-olds). Use the stories as a springboard for discussing family relationships in terms of the children's own families.

TELLING THE STORY

Joseph and His Brothers

Joseph, his eleven brothers, and one sister were growing up. His father and his father's wives took care of Joseph because his mother was dead. Joseph had become a handsome young man. He was now seventeen years old.

Each day Joseph and his ten older brothers took their sheep to graze in the fields near their home. They spent the day watching over the sheep to keep them from wandering away. Each evening when they came back from the fields, Joseph told Jacob about all the things that had happened that day.

Jacob loved all of his children, but he had a special feeling for Joseph. One day he said to Joseph, "I have a present for you. It's a beautiful coat with stripes."

Joseph was surprised and happy. He said, "Father, I've never seen such a fancy coat! I'll wear it all the time so that everyone will see it and know how much you love me."

Joseph was proud of his new coat. He wore it all the time. When his brothers saw him wearing it, they were jealous. They wished that Jacob had made them coats like Joseph's.

One night Joseph had an unusual dream. The next day he gathered his brothers together and said, "I had a really interesting dream. I was in the field with all of you. We were tying bundles of wheat together. The wheat that I tied into a bundle suddenly stood up by itself. Then the wheat that you tied into bundles stood up, too. Your wheat made a circle around mine and bowed down to my wheat."

His brothers were very angry. "Do you mean to rule over us?" they said. "Is that what your dream means?"

Joseph had another dream. He shared it with his brothers and his father. "In this dream the sun, the moon, and eleven stars all bowed down to me." This time his father, too, became angry with him. "Do you think that I and my wives and your brothers should bow down to you? Do you think you're better than we are?"

"Everyone seems so angry with me," thought Joseph, but he still thought about his dreams. He wondered, "Will those dreams really come true?"

Questions on the Story

1. How did wearing the striped coat make Joseph feel?
2. Why do you think Joseph wanted to tell his brothers about his dreams?
3. Why were his brothers angry when they heard about the dreams?

In the Fields

One day Jacob said to Joseph, "Your brothers went to Shechem with the sheep. Please go and find them."

Joseph thought to himself, "My brothers are very angry and upset with me. They're just jealous because father made me a beautiful new coat and because I told them about my dreams. I don't want to go to Shechem to look for them. But I should do what Father asks me to do. He is my father and I love him so much." So he said to Jacob, "I'm ready to go if you want me to."

Joseph put on his beautiful coat. He got his things together. As he was leaving, Jacob called to him, "See if everything is well with your brothers and with the sheep. Then come back here and tell me."

Joseph walked and walked a long time. He wondered where his brothers might be. When he got closer to Shechem, he wasn't sure if he was going in the right direction. He wandered across a field and saw a man in the distance. The man called to him, "What are you looking for?"

"I'm looking for my brothers," said Joseph. "Do you know where they might be with their flock of sheep?"

"They've left here," the man said. "I heard them say, "Let's go to Dotan." Then Joseph walked until he saw his brothers and the sheep in the distance.

The brothers looked up and saw him coming closer. Asher shouted, "Look! Here comes Joseph the dreamer in his special coat."

"I wonder what he wants," Dan said.

"He's just looking for trouble!" Naphtali grumbled. "Why doesn't he just leave us alone?"

And Judah said, "Those dreams of his really annoy me. Let's teach him a lesson so that he'll stop bothering us. Let's put him into that pit over there."

Reuben heard what his brothers said. He was worried. He thought to himself, "I am the oldest. Father says that I am responsible for my brothers. If Joseph doesn't come home with us today, Father will be very upset. I'll try to convince the others not to hurt Joseph. After they've left and gone home, I'll pull Joseph out of the pit." Then Reuben said to his brothers, "Let's be careful not to hurt Joseph. We can teach him a lesson, but let's not hurt him." Then he wandered off to see how the sheep were doing in the field.

As Joseph came closer to his brothers, they grabbed him, pulled off his beautiful coat, and threw him into a deep, empty pit. He tried and tried to get out, but he couldn't do it.

Questions on the Story

1. Why were Joseph's brothers upset with him?
2. How were Joseph's brother going to teach him a lesson?
3. Why was the oldest brother, Reuben, worried about what his brothers were going to do with Joseph?
4. What do you think is going to happen to Joseph? To Reuben? To the other brothers?
5. What kind of a person was Joseph? (5 and 6-year-olds)

The Caravan

All of the brothers then sat down to eat bread and to rest. As they were sitting and resting and talking, they noticed something way off in the distance. Asher said, "I wonder what that can be?"

"It looks like a caravan of camels and men," said Levi. "They must be taking things to Egypt to sell."

Judah said, "I have an idea. It wouldn't be right to hurt Joseph. After all, he is our brother. Let's sell him to those men who are going to Egypt. Then we can get rid of him and he won't bother us anymore."

Gad yelled to the men in the caravan. "Would you like to pay us for a helper who will work for you?"

"Sure," said one of the men. "We need a helper and we can pay you for him."

Then the men pulled Joseph out of the pit. They paid the brothers and they set off for Egypt with Joseph.

As the brothers watched the caravan leave, Reuben came back. He thought, "Joseph has learned his lesson. Now I'll pull him out of the pit and take him home."

But what a big surprise he got when he looked into the pit. "Oh my goodness, oh no, oh no!" he yelled. He looked all around. "Joseph's gone! What will I tell Father? Oh no! He'll blame me if I don't bring Joseph home!"

Then the brothers told him what they had done. They looked off in the distance and saw that the caravan had disappeared from sight. It was too late!

The brothers began to feel sorry for what they had done. They said to each other, "What will we tell Father? What can we say? Father loves Joseph so much. He'll be so upset. We won't be able to make him feel better."

Suddenly one of them said, "I have a good idea! Let's tell Father that a wild animal attacked Joseph while he was in the field."

"That's a good idea," said the others. They took Joseph's coat and dipped it into the blood of a goat. When they returned home, they showed it to Jacob. They told him a story that wasn't true.

"Look what we found, Father," they said. "This looks like Joseph's coat. Do you really think it is his?"

Jacob looked at it and cried in a loud voice, "It is Joseph's coat. A wild animal must have killed him."

Jacob was very, very sad. He cried and cried. The brothers felt very, very sorry inside, but they didn't know how to tell their father the truth.

Questions on the Story

1. How do you think Joseph felt when his brothers threw him into the pit?
2. How did Joseph feel when the men going to Egypt took him away?
3. Were Joseph's brothers sorry for the way they treated him? Why?
4. What did Joseph's brothers tell their father? Should they have told him the truth?

On to Egypt

Meanwhile the men in the caravan were taking Joseph to Egypt. "Let's sell him to an important person in Egypt," they said to each other, "then we can make a lot of money." And that was what they did. They sold him to Potiphar, who managed Pharaoh's large household.

Potiphar was a very rich man and he owned many things. He had many workers in his home. Joseph became one of them. Potiphar liked Joseph very much. He liked the way Joseph looked, he liked the way he spoke, and he liked the way he acted. He put Joseph in charge of his house and everything in it.

Joseph felt very lucky to live in Potiphar's house. He thought to himself, "Even though my brothers were so mean to me and I miss my father, everything seems good for me now. How can I be so lucky to have such a good life here in Egypt? I know that God is helping me. God has blessed Potiphar's house and everything in it. God is helping me because God wants me to be happy and successful."

Questions on the Story

1. How do you think Joseph felt being in Egypt?
2. Do you think Joseph missed his father? His brothers?
3. Who was helping Joseph?

THEMES IN THE STORY

The Relationship Between Joseph and His Brothers

Joseph was the favored son. He flaunted this over his brothers with the result that they were very antagonistic toward him.

Bringing the Theme Closer

- How does it feel when one child gets a present and others don't?
- What does jealous mean? Have you ever been jealous? Encourage discussion.
- What should you do when you feel jealous?
- Develop a conversation about Joseph's behavior toward his brothers.

Jacob and Joseph

The relationship between Jacob and Joseph was unique. Because Joseph was Rachel's firstborn son, he was favored by Jacob.

Bringing the Theme Closer
- How do you think Joseph felt at being singled out as a "special son"?
- Ask the children to think of certain times when a child is special to a parent (on a birthday, when the child is in a performance at school, at graduation, etc.). Discuss how it feels at those special times.

Joseph's Dreams

Joseph's dreams reinforced his feeling of being special, of being better than his brothers.

Bringing the Theme Closer
- What did Joseph dream?
- Why did this dream make Joseph think that he was "better" than his brothers?
- Why do you think that Joseph told his dreams to his brothers even though they didn't like him? Is it possible that he didn't know how much the others disliked him?
- If you were Joseph, would you have told your brothers about your dreams?
- Do you ever have dreams? Who do you tell about your dreams?
- Can you tell the class about one of your dreams?

The Brothers Sell Joseph

The brothers wanted to take revenge on Joseph, but in so doing, they hurt Jacob. When we hurt one person, we may hurt many people.

Bringing the Theme Closer
- What should someone do when he or she has done something wrong? Should the person tell someone about it?
- Discuss the idea that when we hurt one person, we hurt many people.

CREATIVE FOLLOW-UP

Retelling the Story

Goals

To help children sequence the events of the story.
To help children understand the emotions/feelings of all the story characters.

PAPER PLATE MASKS (3 AND 4-YEAR-OLDS)

Description of Activity

Children describe feelings through the use of masks.

Materials

large paper plates, one for each child
tongue depressors
stapler
felt markers

Procedure

1. Before class, make a paper plate mask for each child. Staple each paper plate onto a tongue depressor. Draw a different emotion/feeling on each plate (e.g. anger, joy, sadness, sorrow, puzzlement). See diagram below:

2. Review the story with the children, emphasizing the way each of the people felt.
3. Show the children the already made paper plate masks.
4. As each character is discussed, either by teacher or children, the paper plate which shows that emotion/feeling is raised.

PAPER PLATE MASKS (5 AND 6-YEAR-OLDS)

Description of Activity
Children describe feelings through the use of masks.

Materials

large paper plates, one for each child
tongue depressors
stapler
felt marker

Procedure
1. Review the story with the children, emphasizing the way each of the characters felt.
2. Let each child talk about one character and the way that person felt.
3. Each child then makes a paper plate depicting that particular emotion/feeling.
4. Encourage the children to share their paper plate masks and to describe the emotion/feeling it shows.

Story Time

Goals
To help the children deal with difficult situations.
To help the children understand the feelings of others.

READ AND DISCUSS (3 AND 4-YEAR-OLDS)

Description of Activity
Children think of solutions for difficult situations.

Materials
If It Weren't for Benjamin: (I'd Always Get To Lick The Spoon) by Barbara Shook Hazen

Procedure

1. Read *If It Weren't for Benjamin: (I'd Always Get To Lick The Spoon)*, which is about sibling rivalry. Encourage a discussion of how people feel when they have arguments, and what they can do to make up.

READ AND DISCUSS (5 AND 6-YEAR-OLDS)

Description of Activity

Read and discuss a story about making a mistake.

Materials

The How: Making the Best of a Mistake by Pauline and Selma Boyd

Procedure

1. Read *The How: Making the Best of a Mistake,* which is about the aftermath of a mistake. Talk about what to do when a mistake is made.

Music and Dance

Goals

To reinforce specific parts of the story.
To learn the song about Joseph.

CREATIVE MOVEMENT (3 AND 4-YEAR-OLDS)

Description of Activity

Children move creatively to a song about Jacob.

Materials

tape recorder
song: "Jacob Had Twelve Sons" on the cassette tape *Bible People Songs* by Jeff Klepper
balloons of various colors

Procedure

1. Play the song "Jacob Had Twelve Sons."
2. Encourage the children to move to music while waving the balloons.

CREATIVE MOVEMENT (5 AND 6-YEAR-OLDS)

Description of Activity

Children move creatively to a song about Jacob.

Materials

tape recorder
song: "Jacob Had Twelve Sons" on the cassette tape *Bible People Songs* by
    Jeff Klepper
balloons of various colors

Procedure

1. Choose a leader to move to the music of "Jacob Had Twelve Sons" while
   waving balloons.
2. The other children follow the leader's movements.
3. After a few moments, stop the music and allow the leader to choose a
   replacement.
4. Continue in this way until all the children have been given a chance to
   lead.

TAKING THE STORY HOME

1. Ask parents to read one or both of the following books with their child:
   I Have Feelings by Terry Berger and *Feelings* by Terry Berger. Children then
   describe a character in the story who expressed an emotion described in the
   story.
2. Send home a picture out of which parents can make a puzzle with their
   child, and a manilla envelope in which to keep the pieces. The child glues the
   picture onto cardboard and colors it using felt markers. The parent
   laminates the picture, then cuts it into pieces (2-6 pieces for 3 and 4-year-
   olds, 8-10 pieces for 5 and 6-year-olds). Suggest that parent and child discuss
   the story as the puzzle is put together.
3. Send home a list of story starters for children to complete. Examples follow:
   * Joseph was surprised by his dream because . . .
   * Joseph's brothers didn't want to hear about his dreams because . . .
   * Jacob was angry at Joseph when . . .
   * Joseph went out to the field to . . .
   * Joseph's brothers threw him in the pit so that . . .
   * When Reuben came back and Joseph was not in the pit, Reuben . . .

CHAPTER 9

Joseph in Prison

BEFORE TELLING THE STORY

1. Review with the children Joseph's boyhood in Canaan and his arrival in Egypt.
2. Discuss with the children Joseph's attitude toward and relationship with his father and brothers. Compare this relationship to his relationship with Potiphar and his household. Ask children what Joseph might have liked/not liked about his father, about his brother, about Potiphar and his household.

TELLING THE STORY

Joseph in Potiphar's House

Joseph was now in charge of all the work and workers in Potiphar's house and fields.

Joseph was a good leader. He taught the workers how to do the work. He told the workers when their work was good. He helped them when the work was hard. All the workers liked Joseph. Potiphar was very happy with Joseph. He told Joseph, "You are the best man I have ever had in charge of my house. I am proud of you and your work!"

Joseph thought, "God has helped me and that's why everything is working so well!"

Potiphar's wife had a problem with Joseph. She wanted Joseph to spend time with her, but Joseph refused. This made her very angry. She told Potiphar things about Joseph that were not true. She said, "Joseph is in charge of all the work in this house, but he is not what he seems to be. And he is not nice to me."

Potiphar was surprised, but he believed his wife. He was furious. He went to Joseph and said, "I am disappointed. I always trusted you. Now my wife tells me bad things about you."

Joseph couldn't believe what he heard. "I'm sorry that there is a problem," he said, "but what she has told you is not true." Still, Potiphar believed his wife and sent Joseph to prison.

Questions on the Story

1. What do you think Joseph's jobs were in Potiphar's house and fields?
2. Why do you think Joseph was chosen as head of Potiphar's workers, as well as of his house and fields?
3. Why did Potiphar's wife tell Potiphar things about Joseph that were not true? Why do you think Potiphar chose to believe her? (5 and 6-year-olds)
4. How do you think Joseph felt when he was sent to prison?

Joseph in Prison

Joseph was upset and afraid. At first he just sat by himself in the prison. He kept thinking about his father and his brothers and all the things that had happened to him.

After a while he started to meet the other prisoners. Then he became friends with them. He loved to talk with them, to tell them stories and to give them advice. Sometimes when the prisoners argued among themselves, Joseph found a way to settle their arguments. The prisoners liked him. "Joseph is very smart," they said to each other, "he always knows the right thing to do. He is a good friend."

The man in charge of the prison liked Joseph, too. One day he said, "From now on, Joseph, you will be in charge of the prisoners. You will help them with their problems." Joseph liked his new job. The prisoners were happy, too. Joseph took good care of them.

Two of the prisoners had been helpers to the Pharaoh. One man had been in charge of all the wines in the palace. He had been the chief butler. The second man was the chief baker. He was in charge of all the baking in the palace. They had important jobs, but now they were in prison. Pharaoh was angry with them for not doing their job well.

One morning Joseph met the chief butler and the chief baker. They were sitting alone, looking troubled. "Did something happen?" asked Joseph.

The chief butler answered, "We both had strange dreams last night. We don't understand them, and we have no one who can tell us what they mean."

Joseph smiled and said, "God understands dreams. Tell them to me. Maybe God will help me to understand what they mean."

The two men didn't know whether to believe Joseph or not. Joseph said, "Come on, tell me. I once had strange dreams and I understood them. Let me hear about yours."

The men finally agreed to tell their dreams. The chief butler went first. Joseph listened carefully. For a long time he didn't say anything. "Well," said the butler, "I knew you wouldn't understand my dream."

"I will explain the dream," said Joseph. "Sit down and listen. In three days Pharaoh will take you out of here and back to his palace. You will again serve him wine just as you did before you were sent to prison."

The eyes of the chief butler lit up and he said to Joseph, "Do you mean that I will really be free and that I will again be the chief butler?" "Yes," said Joseph, "and it will happen in three days."

The chief butler was smiling. He asked, "How can I pay you?"

"You don't have to pay me," said Joseph. "I have only a small favor to ask you."

"Anything you want," said the chief butler. "Just ask."

"When you return to the palace, talk to Pharaoh about me. Maybe he will let me out of this place."

"Sure," said the chief butler. "You can be sure that I will talk to the Pharaoh about you."

Then it was the chief baker's turn to tell his dream. "Please, listen to my dream, too, and tell me what it means," he said.

"I am ready," said Joseph. When the baker finished speaking, he waited. Joseph was silent again. "Well," asked the chief baker, "what does it mean? Will Pharaoh let me go, too?"

Joseph shook his head. "Your dream is different. In three days you will leave this prison, but you will not go back to the palace. Pharaoh will not want you back." The chief baker was very upset. He wished he could go back to Pharaoh's palace.

One day passed. Two days passed. The third day was Pharaoh's birthday. Pharaoh made a big party for all his people. He ordered that the chief baker and the chief butler be brought out of prison in honor of his birthday. Just as Joseph had said, the chief butler went back to his old job. What a happy chief butler he was! And just as Joseph had said, the chief baker did not go back to his old job.

Joseph stayed in prison. He hoped that the chief butler would remember his promise to talk about him to Pharaoh. He waited and waited.

Questions on the Story

1. Why was Joseph chosen to be in charge of all the prisoners?
2. Why did Joseph think he could help the chief butler and chief baker understand their dreams?
3. What did Joseph ask the chief butler to do for him when the chief butler returned to Pharaoh's palace?
4. How did Pharaoh celebrate his birthday?

THEMES IN THE STORY

Joseph – An Unusual and Clever Man

Joseph is a very unique and complex individual.

Bringing the Theme Closer
- What was Joseph like? Was he a nice person? How do you know?
- What kind of person makes a good leader? Was Joseph a good leader? A good friend? A good interpreter of dreams?

The Dreams of the Butler and the Baker

The dreams in this story are symbolic of events to come.

Bringing the Theme Closer
- What do you think the chief butler's dream was all about?
- Do you think all dreams come true? Have you ever had a dream come true?

CREATIVE FOLLOW-UP

Retelling the Story

Goals

To help the children to sequence the events of the story.
To encourage understanding and internalization of the feelings of the story characters.

BALL PUPPETS (3 AND 4-YEAR-OLDS)

Goals

To help the children to understand and internalize the feelings of the characters in the story.

Description of the Activity

Children discuss situations and feelings through the use of ball puppets.

Materials

one half sheet newspaper
square pieces of white fabric (or a man's handkerchief), one for each child
buttons
grosgrain ribbon
yarn
felt markers
white glue

Procedure

1. Review the story with the children.
2. Invite each child to talk about one character in the story and the feelings of that character.
3. Gather a group of 4 or 5 children together to make ball puppets.

4. Have each child crumple one half sheet of newspaper into a tight ball.
5. Help each child to place his/her ball into the center of a piece of fabric and close the fabric around it.
6. To form the head of the puppet, tie a strip of grosgrain ribbon around the fabric-covered ball, leaving space underneath for insertion of two or more fingers.
7. Children may decorate the puppets with buttons, yarn, grosgrain ribbon, and felt markers as desired.
8. Encourage the children to share their puppets and to describe the emotions/feelings they show.

BOTTLE PEOPLE (5 AND 6-YEAR-OLDS)

Description of Activity

Children review in detail feelings of particular characters in the story as they create bottle people.

Materials

detergent bottle
white glue
buttons
sparkles
felt markers
yarn
fabric
scissors

Procedure

1. Following the initial storytelling, discuss the characters and their feelings.
2. Carefully wash the detergent bottle.
3. Invite a small group of children to a table where the above materials are easily accessible. Encourage each child to use the materials to create a "bottle person" in the form of a biblical story character.
4. Continue this project with additional groups until all of the children have had an opportunity to participate. (This project can extend over several days if desired.)
5. During circle time, those who have completed bottle people can display them at appropriate times during the retelling of the story.

6. Encourage the children to discuss the feelings of their story character in detail during the creation of the bottle person. The teacher or a child then retells the story. As a story character is being described, the child whose bottle person is of that character's face, holds up his/her bottle person and tells the class about that character's feelings. This procedure can continue until the completion of the story.

Discussion

Goals

To understand the role of dreams in this story.
To acquire information about dreams.

READ AND DISCUSS (3 AND 4-YEAR-OLDS)

Description of Activity

Read and discuss stories about dreams.

Materials

Where the Wild Things Are by Maurice Sendak and *In The Night Kitchen* by Maurice Sendak.

Procedure:

1. Read one or more of the following books: *Where the Wild Things Are* by Maurice Sendak and *In the Night Kitchen* by Maurice Sendak.
2. Discuss the books, then talk about dreams which the children might have had.

EXPERIENCE CHARTS (5 AND 6-YEAR-OLDS)

Description of Activity

Children discuss dreams through the use of an experience chart.

Materials

newsprint paper
magic marker

Procedure

1. Ask questions such as the following: When do you dream? Who or what is in your dream(s)? Describe something about your dream(s). Do you like to dream? Is it fun to dream? Is it scary? How else would you describe dreams?
2. Write the children's responses on experience charts.
3. Each child is given his/her experience chart to decorate and take home.

Music and Dance

Goal

To help the children to sequence the events of the story.

SING AND SWAY (3 AND 4-YEAR-OLDS)

Description of Activity

Children move creatively to a song.

Materials

tape recorder
song: "Joseph You're a Dreamer" from the cassette tape *Bible People Songs* by Jeff Klepper

Procedure

1. Play the song "Joseph You're a Dreamer."
2. Choose a child to be the leader. The child moves to the music as the others follow his/her movements. When the teacher stops the music, the child chooses another leader. The children follow the movements of that child until the music stops again.
3. Continue this procedure until each child has had a turn as leader.

SING AND SWAY (5 AND 6-YEAR-OLDS)

Description of Activity

Children dramatize a song through creative movement.

Materials

tape recorder
song: "Joseph You're a Dreamer" from the cassette tape *Bible People Songs*
    by Jeff Klepper

Procedure

1. Choose one child to be Joseph. The child moves to the music of "Joseph You're a Dreamer" doing something that Joseph did in the story.
2. The other children try to guess what action the child is demonstrating.
3. The child who guesses correctly gets a turn to be Joseph.

Cooking

Goals

To help children understand the role of a beautifully set table and tasty food in a celebration.

To help children understand how important it was for servants to please the ruler with food.

A KING'S PARTY (3 AND 4-YEAR-OLDS)

Description of Activity

Children decorate desserts "fit for a king."

Materials

prepared icing
sprinkles
spatula
cake plate, cake rack
cookie sheet
waxed paper
paper plates
chocolate chips
prepared cookies
sheet cake cut into squares (one for each child)

Procedure

1. Discuss the role of food in a celebration and the importance of food to rulers such as Pharaoh.
2. During free play time, take 3-4 children at a time to a table set up with materials for decorating cookies and a cake.
3. Instruct each child to wash his/her hands before proceding to decorate.
4. Give each child a paper plate with a piece of wax paper on it. Children choose and decorate two cookies or a piece of cake, or all three.
5. Refrigerate the cookies and pieces of cake, and call another group.
6. Prepare this snack "fit for a king" early in the week and serve it at the pre-Shabbat party.
7. Teach children the blessing recited before eating baked goods:

   Baruch Atah Adonai Eloheynu Melech Ha'olam Borey Miney M'zonot. Blessed are You O Eternal our God Ruler of the universe who creates various kinds of foods.

A KING'S PARTY (5 AND 6-YEAR-OLDS)

Description of Activity

Children make goblets "fit for a king" and use them at "A King's Party."

Materials

plastic disposable wine glasses, one for each child
sparkles
glue
Q-tips
grape juice

Procedure

1. Provide each child with a plastic wine glass.
2. With a Q-tip, each child paints the glue onto his/her wine glass. (Instruct children to keep the glue on the lower half of the glass so that it doesn't interfere with drinking from it.)
3. Each child sprinkles sparkles onto the glass, choosing the colors that appeal to him/her.
4. Set the glasses aside to dry.
5. When the glasses are dry, have a "King's Party." Serve grape juice in the king's goblet and fancy cookies.
6. Recite the *Kiddush* and the blessing over baked goods (see above).

TAKING THE STORY HOME

1. Send the story home. Suggest that parents play *Who Am I?* with the children. Parent gives clues and child guesses who the character is. After a correct guess, the child can give the parent clues. A sample dialogue follows:

   Parent says: "Who am I? I used to live in a very fancy house called a palace."

   Child guesses: "Is it Joseph?"

   Parent says: "Try again. Here's another clue. I bake the best cakes in Egypt."

   Child guesses: "Is it the baker?"

   Parent says: "Right. Now it's your turn."

2. Ask parents to discuss their child's dreams with them over the course of several days. If their child is agreeable, they may write down the dreams for discussion at school.

3. Send home a list of story starters for the children to complete. Examples follow:

   - Potiphar was happy with Joseph because . . .
   - Potiphar's wife told Potiphar that Joseph . . .
   - When Joseph went to prison, the other prisoners thought Joseph was . . .
   - The chief butler told Joseph that in his dream . . .
   - The chief baker was sad because Joseph told him that . . .

CHAPTER 10

Pharaoh's Dream

BEFORE TELLING THE STORY

1. Review Joseph's journey and arrival in Egypt. Also discuss Joseph in prison, how he got there and his position in the prison.
2. Discuss the dreams of the chief butler and chief baker, as well as the interpretations that Joseph offered. Review once again how, when, and where we dream.

The Dreams

Joseph was in prison. He hoped that the chief butler would remember to tell Pharaoh about him. He waited and waited, but nothing happened.

Joseph thought, "The chief butler must have forgotten to speak to Pharaoh about me. What will happen? I want so much to be free. I want to enjoy the sun shining during the day and the moon at night. I want to walk wherever I wish. There are so many things I want to do. Pharaoh is the ruler of Egypt. He can do anything he wants. If he says that I should leave this prison, I can be free." But two years passed, and Joseph stayed in prison.

One night Pharaoh had two dreams. In his dreams he stood near the Nile River. He saw cows walking out of the water. First there was one cow, then another, then another, until there were seven cows – seven big, fat, healthy cows. They walked to the fields to eat.

Then Pharaoh saw seven other cows in his dream. They were walking out of the Nile River, too. But these cows looked thin and scrawny. They walked slowly to the field where the fat cows stood. Suddenly they swallowed the fat cows, but they stayed skinny.

Pharaoh woke up and thought about the dream. He wondered and wondered what it could mean. After a while he got very sleepy. He closed his eyes and dreamed again. This time he saw seven big ears of grain growing in the field. The grain had many kernels and it stood tall and healthy. Then seven thin ears of grain grew up, too. There were very few kernels on those ears of grain. Suddenly the seven thin ears of grain swallowed the seven healthy ears of grain, but they stayed thin.

Pharaoh woke up again. He sat up in his bed thinking, "What could those dreams mean?" He didn't know the answer.

Questions on the Story
1. What did Joseph wish for while he was in prison?
2. What did Joseph want to do when he was free?
3. What do you think Pharaoh's dreams meant? (5 and 6-year-olds)

The Wise Men

Pharaoh called some wise men to his palace. He told them all about his dreams. When he finished he said, "You are the wise men of Egypt. Can you explain what my dreams mean?"

The wise men looked down. They scratched their heads. They shook their heads. They couldn't understand those dreams.

The chief butler was in the room while Pharaoh spoke about his dreams. He said, "Pharaoh, I just remembered someone who can explain your dreams. I was supposed to tell you about him sooner, but I forgot."

Pharaoh was excited. "Tell me about this person," he said. Then the chief butler told Pharaoh all about Joseph. He told Pharaoh that Joseph was able to understand dreams and explain them.

When Pharaoh heard this he said, "I must meet this young Hebrew right away." Then he ordered that Joseph be brought to him.

Joseph was thrilled at the news. He knew that the chief butler had kept his promise. He washed, combed his hair, put on nice clothes, and got ready to meet Pharaoh.

When Joseph stood in front of Pharaoh, the king liked the way he looked. He thought that Joseph looked like a smart young man. He said to Joseph, "I dreamed two strange dreams last night. No one can explain them to me. I heard that you understand dreams, so tell me about mine." And then Pharaoh told Joseph his dreams from beginning to end.

When Pharaoh finished talking Joseph said, "I can explain your dreams. The seven fat cows and seven good ears of grain mean seven years of plenty. For seven years there will be lots of food in Egypt. The cows will have plenty to eat. They will grow big and give a lot of milk. Egypt will have much good food."

Pharaoh liked to hear this. He smiled. Then Joseph said, "The seven thin cows and seven thin ears of grain mean seven bad years. There will not be much food in Egypt during those years. There won't be crops growing in the fields, so the cows won't have much to eat. They will become thin and they won't give much milk."

Pharaoh looked worried now. He thought for a few moments. Then he said, "But I don't understand why the skinny cows swallowed the fat cows and yet they stayed skinny. And the thin ears of grain swallowed the fat ears of grain and they stayed thin. What does that mean?"

Joseph answered, "When the seven bad years will come, things will be so bad in the land of Egypt that the people will not remember the seven good years. It will be as if there never were seven good years. God was letting you know that the seven good years begin now. Now is the time to plan for the bad times to come."

Pharaoh was really worried now. He asked, "What can I do to help my people?"

Joseph answered, "You must choose a smart man who will gather grain from all over Egypt during the seven good years. The grain will be put in storage places for the seven bad years. If you do this, then there will be food to eat during the seven bad years."

Pharaoh smiled at Joseph. He liked him even more than he did when he first saw him. "I think you are the man to do this job. You are smart and I am sure that you will be able to do it well."

Questions on the Story

1. Could Pharaoh understand his own dreams? Why not?
2. Why did Pharaoh let Joseph out of prison?

3. Do you think Pharaoh's dreams will come true? Why do you think so?

4. How did Pharaoh know that Joseph was smart?

THEMES IN THE STORY

Joseph Interprets Pharaoh's Dreams

Joseph had the unusual ability to interpret dreams and then to use them to foretell the future. Pharaoh was impressed with Joseph's unique gift.

Bringing the Theme Closer
- How are the two dreams of Pharaoh alike? (5 and 6-year-olds)
- Why do you think Pharaoh had two such similar dreams? (5 and 6-year-olds)
- What did Pharaoh think when Joseph told him what his dreams meant? (5 and 6-year-olds)

The Dreams

Joseph had several experiences with dreams – as a dreamer and as an interpreter. When discussing Joseph and dreams, encourage the children to ask and respond freely to their own questions about dreams.

Bringing the Theme Closer
- What did Joseph's brothers say about him when they heard his dreams?
- Was Joseph a special person? Why?
- Do you like Joseph? Why?
- Do you know people like Joseph? Tell us about them.
- Could Joseph understand his own dreams? Refer back to young Joseph as he told his brothers about his dreams. (5 and 6-year-olds)

CREATIVE FOLLOW-UP

Retelling the Story

DISCUSSION (3 AND 4-YEAR-OLD)

Goals

To help the children sequence the events of the story.
To help the children to interpret the events of the story on their level.

Description of Activity

The children's understanding of the story is expanded through visual materials.

Materials

pictures of cows
ears of grain
pictures of wheat fields

Procedure

1. Show the pictures and stalks of wheat (dried) to the children.
2. Ask the children to relate the pictures to the story sequentially. As you are showing the pictures and the wheat, the children take turns telling what they remember of the story.

EXPERIENCE CHARTS (5 AND 6-YEAR-OLDS)

Goals

To help the children sequence the events of the story.
To help the children to interpret the events of the story on their level.
To help children understand planning and conserving.

Description of Activity

Children sequence the events of the story.

Materials

newsprint paper
felt marker

Procedure

1. Elicit information from the children and write their responses on the experience chart. The following subjects are suggested:
   a. What does a good year mean to a farmer?
   b. What does a bad year mean to a farmer?
   c. What can we do when there is not enough water?
   d. What can we do when there is not enough gas for the car?

Game Time

Goals

To focus on the number/counting aspects of the story.
To encourage the children to cooperate and take turns.

MATCHING GAME (3 AND-4-YEAR OLDS)

Description of Activity

Children play the game *Seven Good Years, Seven Bad Years*, matching numbers with the appropriate pictures.

Materials

pictures of fat cows in groups of different sizes from 1 to 7
pictures of skinny cows in different sizes of groups from 1 to 7
pictures of fat ears of grain in different sizes of groups from 1 to 7
pictures of skinny ears of grain in different sizes of groups from 1 to 7

Procedure

1. Before playing, make a game board with 28 spaces (7 spaces across and 4 down as shown in the diagram below):

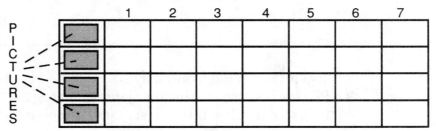

2. Also prepare picture cards of fat and skinny cows, of fat and skinny ears of grain, and of the numbers 1 to 7.
3. Explain the rules of the game to one child or to a pair of children.
4. Encourage the children to match the numbers at the top of the board with the picture cards to the left of the board until all the boxes are filled in.

SEVEN GOOD YEARS, SEVEN BAD YEARS (5 AND 6-YEAR-OLDS)

Description of Activity

The children play a game which focuses on the story and on the number 7.

Materials

game board
spinner
four plastic discs (of different colors)
picture cards showing a fat cow, a skinny cow, a fat ear of grain, a skinny ear
    of grain

Procedure

1. Make the game board (see illustration below).

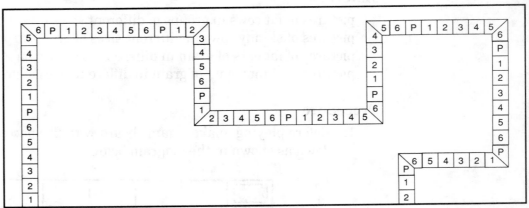

P = Picture

2. Two to four children may play.
3. Players take turns using the spinner and moving their disc to the indicated number. If the player lands on seven and has a matching picture, he/she gets an extra turn.

4. Upon completion of a turn, the player picks a picture card from the pile and keeps it.
5. The child who finishes first is the winner.

Song Time

Goals

To reinforce the events of the story.
To help develop a feeling of accomplishment in the area of music.

SING AND SHOW (3 AND 4-YEAR-OLDS)

Description of Activity

Children make up and dramatize verses on the events of the story.

Materials

Procedure

1. Teacher and children stand in a circle. Together they sing a verse about events of the story to the tune of "Here We Go 'Round the Mulberry Bush." An example follows:

    "This is the dream that Pharaoh had,
    That Pharaoh had, that Pharaoh had,
    This is the dream that Pharaoh had,
    When he was in his palace."

2. Choose one child to walk around in the center of the circle and lead the other children and the teacher in singing about the story. This verse might be, "This is the way the fat cows walked." The child in the center dramatizes how the fat cows walked and the other children follow.
3. The child in the center chooses another child to enter the circle and sing the next verse (e.g., "This is the way the fat cows eat," "This is the way the thin cows walked," etc.) while leading the others in song.
4. Continue in this manner until all the children have had a chance to be in the circle.

SING AND SHOW (5 AND 6-YEAR-OLDS)

Description of Activity

Each child makes up and dramatizes verses on the story as other children follow and guess who the song is about.

Materials

Procedure

1. The teacher starts singing a verse related to a character in the story to the tune of "Here We Go 'Round the Mulberry Bush" (e.g., "I was called to Pharaoh's palace").
2. The children try to guess who the song is about. The child who guesses correctly sings another verse relating to a character in the story.
3. Continue until all children have had a chance to lead a verse.

Building/Creating

Goals

To encourage the children to express their mental images of the story through a plastic art.

To encourage the children to share their impressions of the story with each other.

CREATE A PICTURE (3 AND 4-YEAR-OLDS)

Description of Activity

Children create a picture based on their ideas of the story, then share it with their classmates.

Materials

pieces of yarn in different colors cut in varying lengths
white glue
scissors
Q-tips
construction paper in a variety of colors

Procedure

1. Review the story with the children.
2. Arrange all materials so that they are easily accessible. Invite the children to use the materials in small groups during free choice time.
3. Encourage the children to glue yarn pieces onto construction paper. Let them choose the pieces of yarn themselves. (You might suggest that they use black yarn on white paper for Joseph in prison.)
4. Children show and describe their pictures to the rest of the class.
5. If necessary, extend this activity over 2 or 3 days so that each child may participate in a small group.

CREATE A PICTURE (5 AND 6-YEAR-OLDS)

Description of Activity

Children create a picture based on their ideas of the story, then share it with their classmates.

Materials

construction paper in a variety of colors
scraps of colored paper cut in different shapes
white glue
scissors
felt markers, one for each child

Procedure

1. Review the story with the children.
2. Arrange all materials so that they are easily accessible and invite the children to use them in small groups during free choice time.
3. For each child prepare a piece of construction paper with a scrap of colored paper glued to it.
4. Encourage each child to select a piece of this paper and a felt marker. Ask children to describe something in the story of which the shape on the paper reminds them. They may then add to the picture using the felt marker to show that item more clearly.
5. Children show and describe their pictures to the class.

TAKING THE STORY HOME

1. Parents take their children to visit a farm. Arrange this by calling the Agricultural Extension Service of a local state university, a local office of the Department of Agriculture, or a local 4-H Club.
2. Parents encourage their child to share information on their dreams. Parents write down what their child says. The child draws pictures of his/her dreams which parents then put in a booklet.
3. Send home a list of story starters for children to complete. Examples follow:
   - Pharaoh called some wise men to his palace to ask them about . . .
   - Pharaoh liked the way Joseph looked because . . .
   - Pharaoh's first dream had seven fat cows which . . .
   - Pharaoh's dream was also about seven thin cows and. . .
   - Joseph told Pharaoh that his dreams meant that . . .

CHAPTER 11

Joseph: A Leader in Egypt

BEFORE TELLING THE STORY

1. Review with the children the events in Joseph's life so far: his boyhood when he flaunted his special relationship with his father in front of his brothers, and his young adulthood when he became a responsible and sensitive person and a leader in Egypt.
2. Discuss how Joseph's experiences helped to shape the person he became (e.g., he was thrown into a pit, sold into slavery, was unjustly thrown into prison, and then was chosen for a position of leadership). Talk about what Joseph might have been like if he hadn't had these experiences.
3. Explain that in time of famine there is a scarcity of food, causing people to be very hungry. Ask children if they have ever been hungry. Discuss what it is to be really hungry in a time of famine. Talk about what we can do to help hungry people today (e.g., provide food, set up shelters, give money, etc.).

TELLING THE STORY

Seven Good Years, Seven Bad Years

Joseph helped Pharaoh to understand his two dreams. Pharaoh said, "Joseph you will be in charge of all the food in Egypt during the seven good years and the seven bad years. Be sure that during those years all the people have food."

Joseph listened. He said to himself, "I have an idea. During the seven good years, we will be able to grow more food than we need. We'll save some of that food in storehouses so that during the seven bad years we'll have enough food. I think it will work."

Then the seven good years began. Everything was planted and grew well. Fruit grew on the trees in the orchards. Wheat and barley grew in the fields. The sheep and the cattle had as much grass to eat as they wanted. The people had more than enough fruits and vegetables and grains.

Joseph was excited to see the food growing so well. He had his workers build big storehouses so that there would be a place to keep the extra wheat. The workers put the wheat into the storehouses.

They did this the first year, the second year, the third year, the fourth year, the fifth year, the sixth year, and the seventh year. By the end of the seventh year there were many, many storehouses all over Egypt and they were all filled with wheat.

Pharaoh was delighted. He said to Joseph, "Your work is so good that I am going to make you the second most important man in Egypt. I will be the only person in this land who is more important than you."

Then Pharaoh gave Joseph a special ring. Everyone who saw the ring knew that Joseph was second only to the Pharaoh.

Then Pharaoh gave Joseph a new name. "From now on," he said, "people will call you Tzafnat Panayach." From that time on, Joseph wore special clothes and rode in a special chariot so that everyone could see how important he was.

Joseph and his wife Asnat and their sons Menasseh and Ephraim were an important family in Egypt.

Then the seven bad years began. Nothing grew in the fields. Nothing grew on the trees in the orchards. Nothing grew at all! There was a famine.

The people in Egypt worried. They said to Joseph, "Please help us. You are in charge of the food in Egypt. We can't make bread without flour and we can't make flour without grain. Isn't there something that you can do?"

"Don't worry," said Joseph, "we will have grain during the next seven years. The storehouses are full. You can buy as much as you need."

The people in Egypt were grateful. They bought grain, ground it into flour, and made bread with the flour.

But in other lands, there was no food. There was a famine. In the land of Canaan where Joseph's father and brothers and their families lived there was a famine, too.

Questions on the Story

1. What was Joseph's plan for feeding the people during the seven bad years?
2. Why did Pharaoh make Joseph the second most important man in Egypt?

3. What did Pharaoh give to Joseph?
4. What was Joseph's new name?
5. What do you think of Joseph's plan to save food for the seven bad years? What would you have done if you had been in charge of the food in Egypt? (5 and 6-year-olds)

Famine in Canaan

Jacob called his sons together. "Reuben, Simeon, Levi, Judah, Issachar, Zebulon, Dan, Naphtali, Gad, Asher, and Benjamin," he said, "there is a famine in the land of Canaan. We don't have wheat for flour. We don't have food for our wives and children. I have heard that in the land of Egypt there is a very important man named Tzafnat Panayach. He will sell wheat to anyone who will buy it."

"But, Father," said Reuben, "the wheat that is being sold in Egypt is only for Egyptians. Maybe they won't sell us any because we are Hebrews from the land of Canaan."

"People from other lands are buying wheat from Egypt," said Jacob. "Take some money and some empty sacks, and buy wheat from the important man in Egypt. All of you except Benjamin should go. He must stay here because he is my youngest son."

"We will do whatever you wish, Father," said Jacob's sons, and they began to prepare for the journey.

It was a long trip. The brothers saw many, many people going to Egypt to buy food. There were many hungry people.

When they arrived in Egypt, the brothers went to a storehouse. They saw an important man there selling wheat. He wore fancy clothes. It was Tzafnat Panayach. He was the person they had come to see.

Questions on the Story

1. How did the famine in Canaan change the lives of Jacob and his family? What did Jacob and his sons do when the famine came?

2. Why did Jacob want Benjamin to stay in Canaan with him?
3. What did the brothers see when they arrived in Egypt? Do you think they recognized Joseph?

Joseph and His Brothers

Joseph looked at the people who were buying wheat. Suddenly he saw his brothers in the crowd. They were wearing the same kind of clothing they wore when he last saw them.

The brothers walked toward him. Joseph couldn't stop staring at them. He was excited to see them. He kept looking among them for Benjamin, but Benjamin wasn't there. He wondered, "Where is Benjamin? Do they recognize me? What would they say if I told them that I am Joseph? Would they be pleased to see me? Will they say that they are sorry for selling me to the Egyptians?"

The brothers bowed to Joseph as all of the other people were doing. Then Joseph remembered his dream from a long time ago. In the dream the bundles of wheat that belonged to his brothers bowed down to his bundle of wheat. Then Joseph thought about his other dream in which the sun, moon, and stars bowed down to him. He remembered how angry his brothers were when they heard about his dreams.

Joseph saw that his brothers did not recognize him. He decided not to tell them just yet that he was their brother.

"Where are you from?" he asked one of them.

"We are from Canaan," said the brother. "We came to Egypt to buy wheat because there is no wheat in our land."

Then Joseph said, "I saw you wandering in the city and looking all around. You must be spies."

"Oh, no! We are not spies," said Reuben.

"I don't believe you," answered Joseph.

"Reuben told you the truth," said Judah. "We are Hebrews from Canaan. We are ten of the twelve sons of Jacob. Our youngest brother stayed home. We also had another brother, but he is gone now."

When he heard this, Joseph quickly looked down so that no one would see the tears in his eyes. He wished he could see Benjamin again. He missed him so much!

"If you want to prove to me that you are not spies, you must bring your youngest brother here," he said. "Take some wheat and go home, but one of you must stay here. When you bring your youngest brother to me, I will know that you told me the truth. Then I will free the brother who stayed here."

The brothers had to do as Joseph said. They needed wheat for their families.

They said to each other, "Father will be upset about this. He won't want Benjamin to leave home. We are to blame for this. We sold Joseph. We told our father that a wild animal ate Joseph. Father thinks that Joseph is dead. That's why he won't want to let Benjamin go with us."

They didn't notice that Joseph was listening. Joseph saw how sorry they were for what they had done to him. He turned away so they wouldn't see him crying. When his tears stopped, he turned to them and said, "Leave Simeon here. Go and buy wheat. Then go home and come back quickly with your youngest brother."

Now Joseph told his workers, "Fill up the sacks of the men from Canaan. Also, hide the money they paid in their wheat sacks so that they won't notice it. Give them food for their trip." And that was what the workers did.

The brothers' camels moved very slowly because the sacks they were carrying were heavy. The brothers traveled for many days. They knew that Jacob and Benjamin were waiting for them.

Questions on the Story

1. Why did Joseph want Benjamin to come to Egypt?
2. Why did Joseph want Simeon to stay in Egypt while the other brothers went back home?
3. Did Joseph really think his brothers were spies? What is a spy? What does a spy do? (5 and 6-year-olds)

THEMES IN THE STORY

Joseph Helps the People of Egypt

Joseph, appointed second only to Pharaoh, was able to design a program which would help the people of Egypt during the seven years of famine.

Bringing the Theme Closer
- Joseph had a big problem to solve: how to feed people when nothing was growing. What do you think were some possible solutions to this problem? Do you think Joseph's solution was good? If not, why not?
- What is needed for things to grow?
- How do you feel when you are hungry? How do you think the people of Egypt felt when they couldn't get food?

Joseph Raises a Family in Egypt

Joseph acquired an Egyptian name, Tzafnat Panayach. He married an Egyptian woman and had children.

Bringing the Theme Closer
- Talk about names. Ask children if they know their Hebrew names.
- Describe the differences between Joseph's life as a slave and his life as Tzafnat Panayach – the things he could do, the clothing he wore, where he lived, the foods he ate.
- Do you think Joseph was happy when he got married in Egypt? Do you think he missed his family even more at that time?

Joseph Meets His Brothers

Joseph must have been startled to see his brothers among those who wanted to buy grain. At first he seemed to want to get even with them for selling him to the Egyptians. He accused his brothers of being spies. He insisted that they bring Benjamin to Egypt, and even kept Simeon as a hostage until they returned. Yet, throughout, his love and compassion shows.

Bringing the Theme Closer
- Joseph's brothers went to Egypt because of a famine. Did you ever hear the word famine before?
- Can you imagine what it might be like to be very hungry all the time?
- Why do you think Joseph said that his brothers were spies? What is a spy? Do you think it was right of Joseph to accuse his brothers of being spies?
- Why do you think Joseph recognized his brothers, but they didn't recognize him?
- Why do you think Joseph insisted that the brothers bring Benjamin to Egypt? Did you every miss someone very much?

CREATIVE FOLLOW-UP

Retelling the Story

Goals

To help children understand the sequence of the story.
To help children begin to understand some facts about life in ancient Egypt.

ROLE PLAY (3 AND 4-YEAR-OLDS)

Description of Activity

Children role play various parts of the story.

Materials

a bowl and utensils for grinding grain
clothing like that worn by Egyptians at the time of Joseph
clothing like that worn by Joseph's brothers
throne

Procedure

1. Using props and costumes, have children role play the following situations:
   a. Joseph describing his plan to store food for the seven bad years.
   b. Pharaoh appointing Joseph second in command.
   c. The people of Egypt coming to Joseph asking for food when the seven bad years began.

    d. Jacob sending his sons to Egypt to buy wheat.

    e. The brothers preparing to leave for Egypt.

    f. Joseph not letting his brothers know that he recognized them.

    g. The brothers greeting Joseph and not recognizing him.

ROLE PLAY (5 AND 6-YEAR-OLDS)

Description of Activity

Children role play various parts of the story.

Materials

a bowl and utensils for grinding grain
clothing like that worn by Egyptians at the time of Joseph
clothing like that worn by Joseph's brothers
throne

Procedure

1. Using props and costumes, have children role play the following situations:
    a. Joseph (Tzafnat Panayach) talking to his wife (Asnat) about his plan to help the people of Egypt.
    b. Joseph's sons talking to each other about their father.
    c. The brothers in Egypt looking for storehouses.
    d. Joseph not letting his brothers know that he recognized him.
    e. The brothers greeting Joseph and not recognizing him.
    f. Joseph accusing the brothers of being spies.
2. Following this activity, place the following items in the Bible corner: model of a grain storehouse, pictures of sheaves of wheat, real wheat sheaves, pictures of clothing worn in Egypt (see pictures at the back of this book). Inform children that they may play in the center during free choice time in the week to come.

Building/Creating

Goals

To learn about family relationships in general.
To learn about Joseph's family relationships.

DRAWING PICTURES (3 AND 4-YEAR-OLDS)

Description of Activity

Each child draws a picture of his/her own family.

Materials

felt markers
drawing paper

Procedure

1. Each child draws a picture of his/her own family.
2. Each child describes his/her family to the teacher who writes the description on the drawing.
3. Children share their pictures and explanations with their classmates during circle time.
4. The teacher draws a picture of Joseph's family and describes it to the children. Hang this picture in the Bible corner.

COLLAGE (5 AND 6-YEAR-OLDS)

Description of Activity

Children make collages of different kinds of families.

Materials

magazines
construction paper
white glue
scissors

Procedure

1. Arrange children in small groups.
2. Have children select pictures of families from the magazines, then cut them out and paste them onto construction paper.
3. As children share their pictures during circle time, they describe family relationships (e.g., brother, father, etc.; younger, oldest, etc.).
4. Discuss with the children who was the oldest, the youngest in Joseph's family. Who was the father? Who were the brothers?

CREATE A MODEL (3 AND 4-YEAR-OLDS)

Goals

To reinforce the importance of the storehouse in Egypt at the time of the story.

To help children understand the usefulness of storehouses.

Description of Activity

Children create storehouses out of blocks.

Materials

a large quantity of wooden blocks in a variety of sizes and shapes

small play people

roll of aluminum foil

instant camera and film

pictures of granaries from an encyclopedia

pictures of ancient grain storehouses (see pictures at the back of this book)

paper towel rolls

green construction paper

Procedure

1. In advance, make palm trees out of paper towel rolls painted brown with green construction paper taped to the top (see example below).

2. Show pictures of grain storehouses. Discuss the purpose of storehouses and their importance in Egypt at the time of the story.
3. Expand the block center play area and display pictures of storehouses there.
4. Sit with a small group of children in the block center and begin to build storehouses. Place all the completed storehouses on the floor, adding the Nile River (made out of a length of aluminum foil), as well as small play people and teacher-made palm trees.

5. Keep the structures standing for a few days so that children may continue working on them.
6. Take pictures with an instant camera and display them in the Bible corner.
7. Before removing the structures, discuss whether or not they look like those described in the story.

CREATE A MODEL (5 AND 6-YEAR-OLDS)

Goals

To reinforce the importance of the storehouse in Egypt at the time of the story.

To help children understand the usefulness of storehouses.

Description of Activity

Children create storehouses out of boxes.

Materials

pictures of granaries from an encyclopedia
pictures of ancient grain storehouses (see picture at the back of this book)
large cardboard cartons with tops
small boxes and cartons
oatmeal containers
masking tape
tempera paints
paint brushes

Procedure

1. Show pictures of grain storehouses to children in a small group. Discuss the purpose of storehouses and their importance in Egypt at the time of the story.
2. Place large cardboard cartons, small boxes, oatmeal containers, masking tape, tempera paints, and paint brushes on a table.
3. Encourage each child to tape boxes together to make a storehouse.
4. Have children paint their storehouses.
5. Each child may share information about his/her storehouse with the rest of the class.
6. Invite other groups of children to create storehouses in the same manner.

7. Display all the storehouses in the Bible corner for a week before the children take them home.
8. As follow-up, make a seed board. Mount samples of different grains on poster board. Match each grain with a wrapper from or picture of a product (e.g., match wheat with a bread wrapper; barley, rye, etc., with an oatmeal container).

Sharing With Others

Goals

To help children understand the meaning of *tzedakah*.
To help children learn ways to share with people who are less fortunate than they.

FEED THE HUNGRY (3 AND 4-YEAR-OLDS)

Description of Activity

Children bring canned and boxed foods to school to distribute to those in need.

Materials

a large sturdy box
canned and boxed foods

Procedure

1. Tell children about people in the community who are in need of food. Ask them to bring canned and boxed foods to school to distribute to those in need. Send a note home to parents describing the project and suggesting ways for them and their child to participate.
2. Help children understand the similarity between the help Joseph and Pharaoh provided to people who needed food and the help the class will provide to needy people in their own community.
3. Collect the food each day for a week. Then invite to the class a representative of a group that helps to feed hungry people to describe how the food reaches those in need.

FEED THE HUNGRY (5 AND 6-YEAR-OLDS)

Description of Activity

Children bring canned and boxed foods to school to distribute to those in need.

Materials

large sheet of newsprint paper
dark felt marker
masking tape (or an easel)

Procedure

1. Tape the sheet of newsprint paper to a wall or place it on an easel.
2. Discuss with children the way that Joseph and Pharaoh helped people who needed food.
3. Ask for suggestions of ways to help those in need in the community.
4. List the suggested recipients and ways to help them (e.g., collecting toys and books to give to needy children, collecting canned and boxed foods to give to the hungry, collecting money to buy medical supplies for earthquake or flood victims, etc.).
5. Children discuss the various recipients and through consensus decide on a project to help one group.
6. Collect the toys, books, food, or money. Send a note home to parents describing the project and suggesting ways they and their child might help.
7. Invite a representative from the recipient group to visit and discuss the needs of the recipients and how the materials will reach them.

TAKING THE STORY HOME

1. Suggest to parents that they discuss upcoming family events with their child and that they involve the child in planning the event. Parents can help their child understand the purpose of planning by involving them in making simple lists of plans, such as the following:

Things We Need To Do

Plan a menu.
Make a shopping list.

Go grocery shopping.
Cook our food.

Have parents discuss with their child how Joseph helped Egypt by planning ahead.

2. Encourage parents to create a family tree with their child which the child can then share with classmates. The teacher can show Joseph's family tree as the children show theirs. All family trees can be displayed in the Bible corner.

3. Send home a list of story starters for children to complete. Examples follow:
   - When Joseph was in charge of all the food in Egypt, he needed to make sure that . . .
   - Joseph helped to save food in Egypt by . . .
   - During the seven bad years, the people of Egypt were worried because . . .
   - Joseph wasn't worried during the bad years because. . .
   - When there was a famine in Canaan, Jacob's sons went to Egypt to . . .

CHAPTER 12

The Return to Egypt

BEFORE TELLING THE STORY

1. Review the events of the previous story: the plan to save food for the famine, the brothers' journey to Egypt to buy grain, the demand that the brothers bring Benjamin to Egypt. Discuss Joseph's role in all of this.
2. Talk about the difficulties of traveling in ancient times – the necessary preparations, the hardships along the way, the length of the trips.

TELLING THE STORY

Jacob's Sons Return Home

The brothers traveled for a long time. After a while they stopped to rest. One of the brothers opened his sack to get food for his donkey. "Look!" he cried. "My money has been returned! It is here in my sack with the wheat!"

The nine brothers returned home to Canaan. They were tired, but very glad that they had brought wheat with them. It would be ground into flour. Their families would be able to make bread from the flour.

Jacob sat in front of his tent. He saw his sons in the distance coming closer and closer. He jumped up and called to the people in the tents, "Everyone, come quickly! My sons are back from Egypt."

He laughed and ran to meet them. He hugged them. "I see you have full sacks of grain. Your trip to Egypt has been successful!"

Suddenly he stopped smiling. "Where is Simeon?" he asked. "He's not with you?" The brothers were quiet.

"What happened?" asked Jacob. "Why don't you look at me and tell me?"

Then Judah explained, "Tzafnat Panayach, the second most important man in Egypt, was angry with us. He said we were spies. We told him we were not spies, but just brothers, all sons of Jacob. He kept asking us questions about our home and family. We told him that we came from Canaan. We said that our father is old, that one of our brothers is gone, and that our youngest brother is at home with our father. He said that if we were telling the truth, we must leave Simeon in Egypt. We must go home with the sacks of wheat, but then come back to Egypt with our youngest brother. He wants to see Benjamin with his own eyes! Then he'll let Simeon go."

Then the brothers emptied their sacks. There in each one's sack was the money he had paid for the wheat. Jacob shook his head. He was confused. "Didn't you pay for the wheat?" he asked.

"Of course we did," said all of the brothers. "The workers in Egypt filled our sacks with wheat and then closed them. Do you think they put the money there? Why would they do that?"

"Hm-m, there's something strange about this," said Jacob. "Don't use the money. Take good care of it. It doesn't belong to us."

Jacob was very upset. "Joseph is gone! Simeon's in Egypt! And now you want to take Benjamin away. No! No! Benjamin cannot go."

Questions on the Story

1. Were the brothers glad to be back home? What is it like to come back home after being away?
2. What was the real name of Tzafnat Panayach?
3. What did the brothers think when they opened their sacks and found the money?
4. Why do you think the brothers' money was returned to them? Why do you think Jacob thought it was strange that the brothers' money was returned to them? (5 and 6-year-olds)
5. Why did Jacob want his sons to return the money found in the sacks?
6. What did Jacob say when he learned that Benjamin must go to Egypt if they were to buy more grain from Tzafnat Panayach?

Another Journey

Days passed. Weeks passed. The wheat that was brought from Egypt was ground into flour. Every day some of it was made into bread. There was less and less wheat in the sacks.

When there was only a little wheat left, Jacob told his sons, "You need to go back to Egypt for more wheat. Take some money to pay for it and return the money that you found in your sacks."

"But, Father, Tzafnat Panayach told us not to come back without Benjamin. If we don't take Benjamin with us, we won't be able to buy more wheat or to free Simeon."

Jacob shook his head sadly and looked down. "If anything were to happen to Benjamin I would be very, very upset."

Then Reuben said, "We have to go back to Egypt. We need more food and we must bring Simeon back with us. Father, let Benjamin go with us." Judah then promised to take very good care of Benjamin. "You'll see, we'll bring him back to you," he said.

As Jacob listened he thought, "I can depend upon my sons. They always keep their promises." Then he said, "Take Benjamin. Also take gifts to this important man in Egypt, and don't forget to return the money that you found in the sacks."

The brothers were excited. They would see Simeon again and they would be able to buy wheat for their families. They prepared for the trip.

When they were ready to leave, Jacob blessed them. "God will be with you. God will protect you. You will arrive safely in Egypt and then you will return home healthy and well with Simeon and Benjamin."

It was time to leave. The brothers said good-bye to their father and their families. Then they went off to Egypt for a second time.

Questions on the Story

1. Why do you think Jacob finally decided to let Benjamin go to Egypt with his brothers?
2. Why were the brothers excited about going to Egypt again?
3. What did Judah promise his father?

THEMES IN THE STORY

The Brothers Return

Jacob was elated to see his sons return. But when he discovered that Simeon was still in Egypt and that Benjamin would have to go there, he was deeply concerned. While Jacob's sons were sensitive to his feelings on this issue, they also knew that they had no choice but to take Benjamin back to Egypt with them in order to rescue Simeon.

Bringing the Theme Closer
- What did Jacob think when his sons told him that Simeon had been left in Egypt and that now they wanted to take Benjamin there, too?
- Should Jacob have permitted Benjamin to go to Egypt? What would you have done if you were Jacob?

Finding Money in the Sacks

Finding money in the sacks gives an unexpected turn to the story. This instance provides an opportunity to deal with feelings and moral issues that arise when finding something that belongs to someone else.

Bringing the Theme Closer
- What would you think if you found something in your bedroom that didn't belong to you?
- What would you do about it?
- Did you ever find something that belonged to someone else? What was it? What did you do about it?

CREATIVE FOLLOW-UP

Retelling the Story

Goals

To help children internalize the values discussed in the story.
To help children evaluate difficult situations so that they may make appropriate choices.

CASE STUDIES (3 AND 4-YEAR-OLDS)

Description of Activity
Children respond to contemporary situations based on the story.

Materials
the following case studies

Procedure
1. Encourage children to respond to the following situations:
   a. Bobby came to school and found a yellow pencil in his cubby. He knew it wasn't his. What should he do?
   b. Susan found a lollipop in her coat pocket. It was not hers. What should she do?
   c. The children came to school and found a toy truck in the block area. It was the same yellow truck that they had seen in the class next door the day before. What should they do?

CASE STUDIES (5 AND 6-YEAR-OLDS)

Description of Activity
Children respond to contemporary situations based on the story.

Materials
the following case studies

Procedure
1. Encourage children to respond to the following situations: Emphasize to them the connection with the biblical events.
   a. Danny came home from school. When he opened his book bag, he found a baseball in there. He knew it wasn't his. How did he know? What should he do?
   b. Beth wanted to borrow Joshua's book. Joshua said she could borrow it, but only if she left something of hers until the book was returned. Should Beth do it? What should she leave with Joshua?
   c. On the way home from school, David did something that he knew would upset his mother. He knew he should tell her, but he didn't want to upset her. What should he do?

Science

Goal

To help the children understand the idea of measuring weight with a scale.

SCALES (3 AND 4-YEAR-OLDS)

Description of Activity

Children make and use a scale.

Materials

1 wire hanger
2 empty milk cartons of equal size
string
scissors
items for weighing (small blocks, buttons, stones, etc.)

Procedure

1. Arrange the children in small groups. Provide sufficient materials so that each child can make a scale.
2. Cut an opening (window) in the side of each empty, washed out milk carton.
3. Cut a piece of string in two equal strands.
4. Tie one end of each string to corner of wire hanger.
5. Attach the other end of each string to the top of the milk carton.
6. Hang the scale in a place that is easily accessible to the children (from a window sill or a door knob).
7. Encourage the children to place blocks, buttons, and stones in each side of the scale. Discuss when the scale is balanced and how many items each side holds.

SCALES (5 AND 6-YEAR-OLDS)

Description of Activity

Children compare a variety of scales.

Materials

baby scale
doctor scale
hand-made scale (see the activity immediately above for 3 and 4-year olds)
produce scale
postage scale
bathroom scale
newsprint paper
felt marker
Items to weigh (blocks, buttons, stones, etc.)

Procedure

1. Place the scales and items for weighing in an easily accessible place, encouraging the children to use them during free play time.
2. During circle time, discuss the similarities and differences between the various types of scales.
3. On an experience chart, list the similarities and differences, as follows:

SCALES These Are the Same	SCALES These Are Different

Dramatic Play

Goals

To clarify for the children the events of the story.
To help children understand the feelings of those in the story.

RECORDED INTERVIEWS (3 AND 4-YEAR-OLDS)

Description of Activity

The teacher interviews the children and tape records the interview.

Materials

tape recorder with microphone
blank cassette tapes

Procedure

1. Ten children pretend to be the nine brothers and Jacob.
2. Using a tape recorder, interview them. Children speak into the microphone, responding to such questions as:
   a. How was your trip, brothers?
   b. What is it like to be home?
   c. What happened to Simeon? Why isn't he with you?
   d. Jacob, are you happy to see your sons?
   e. How did you feel, Jacob, when you found out that Simeon was still in Egypt?
   f. Jacob, do you mind sending Benjamin to Egypt?
3. Play the tape for the whole class.
4. Place the tape recorder and tape in the Bible corner for use by children during free play time.
5. Interview different children the next time this activity is introduced.

RECORDED INTERVIEWS (5 AND 6-YEAR-OLDS)

Description of Activity

One child interviews the others in the class while the interview is tape recorded.

Materials

tape recorder with microphone
blank cassette tapes

Procedure

1. One child plays an interviewer. Each other child in the group takes the part of either Jacob or one of the brothers (except for Joseph and Simeon).

2. The interviewer speaks to each of the children and asks such questions as:
   a. What is your name?
   b. What have you been doing?
   c. How do you feel about the famine in Canaan?
   d. (To Jacob) How do you feel about leaving Simeon in Egypt?
   e. (To Jacob) What have you been doing while your sons were in Egypt?
   e. (To a brother) Do you want to go back to Egypt?
3. Record the interviews on a tape recorder.
4. Play the tape for the whole class.
5. Place the tape recorder and tape in the Bible corner for use by children during free play time.
6. Interview different children the next time this activity is introduced.

TAKING THE STORY HOME

1. Parents help their child learn how scales provide information. In the supermarket, a child can place produce on the scale and report the registered numbers. At home, he/she can weigh purchases on a scale and chart the results as follows:

   ```
   2 Bananas — 8 Ounces
   3 Tomatoes — 7 Ounces
   1 Cucumber — 4 Ounces
   ```

   Parents can encourage the child to weigh himself/herself and to keep a weight chart.

DANNY	
Date	Weight
Sep 2	26
Oct. 10	27
Dec. 7	30

2. Following a discussion about the new name Joseph received in Egypt, family members can talk about their English and Hebrew names and the people for whom they were named. Parents of those who do not have Hebrew names can contact the Rabbi or principal to acquire one. A good resource is the book *The Encyclopedia of English-Hebrew First Names* by Alfred Kolatch.

3. Parents make a chart listing the English and Hebrew names of each family member. Children draw a picture next to each name or cut out a magazine picture to put next to the name, as shown in the diagram below:

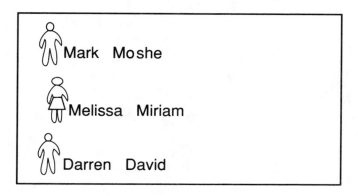

4. Send home a list of story starters for children to complete. Examples follow:
   - The brothers were happy to go home because . . .
   - The brothers were upset that . . .
   - When Asher looked in his sack, he was surprised that. . .
   - Jacob did not want Benjamin to go down to Egypt because . . .
   - Jacob knew that his sons to take Benjamin to Egypt so that . . .

CHAPTER 13

Joseph Tells His Brothers

BEFORE TELLING THE STORY

Review the brothers' first trip to Egypt – how they felt about the journey, how Joseph behaved toward them, how they felt when they left Egypt.

TELLING THE STORY

The Return to Egypt

Joseph's brothers returned to Egypt. Benjamin was with them. They went right away to Tzafnat Panayach's palace. When they got there they were taken to a special room where they stood in front of Joseph.

Joseph looked at his brothers. He saw that Benjamin was with them. He couldn't stop looking at Benjamin. He stayed quiet for a very long time.

Suddenly Joseph said to his chief servant, "Take these people to my house. Tell the cooks to prepare lunch for them. They will eat with me."

The brothers were amazed to be sent to Joseph's house. The last time they met Joseph he had not been kind to them. Now he invited them to eat with him. What could this mean?

Reuben remembered the money that the brothers had found in their sacks. He said to the chief servant, "We want to tell you what happened to us. When we returned home from our last trip to Egypt, we found money in our sacks. It's the money that we paid for the wheat. It's not ours. We don't understand how it got there. But we brought it back. Here, give it to Tzafnat Panayach.

The chief servant smiled. He knew who had put the money into the sacks. "Don't worry," he said.

The brothers were confused. "What does that mean?" they asked each other.

Suddenly Simeon came into the room. The brothers hugged him. The chief servant brought in water so that the brothers could wash

Joseph Tells His Brothers   167

their hands and their feet and gave water to their camels. The brothers felt relaxed. They were glad that they had brought a gift for Joseph.

"Come," called the chief servant. "It is time for lunch."

When the brothers were in the dining room, Joseph entered the room. The brothers bowed to him, because that was the way it was done in Egypt.

"Please accept this gift that our father sent you," said Reuben. "He is old and was not able to come to Egypt."

Joseph looked at each of the brothers until he noticed Benjamin. Then he stared and stared at Benjamin. "Is this your youngest brother, the one you told me about?" he asked.

"Yes, this is our brother Benjamin," said the others.

Joseph thought to himself, "Finally I see my little brother Benjamin whom I missed so much for all these years!"

He was so excited that he thought he might cry. He didn't want his brothers to see him crying so he quickly left the room and went to a private place to cry. When he finished crying, he wiped his eyes. Then he washed his face and calmly went back to the dining room.

"Please serve the food now," Joseph said to his servants. Everyone was smiling happily, but no one was as happy as Joseph. Again, he thought, "There is my little brother Benjamin."

After lunch Joseph called out, "Servants, fill these men's sacks with food." Then very, very quietly he said to one of the servants, "Put my silver cup and this money in the youngest one's sack."

The brothers were very pleased that they would be returning home the next morning.

Questions on the Story

1. What did the brothers think about Tzafnat Panayach? What did Tzafnat Panayach think about them?
2. Why didn't Joseph want to cry in front of his brothers?
3. Why didn't Joseph tell his brothers who he really was?
4. Why do you think Tzafnat Panayach invited the brothers for lunch? How did the brothers feel about having lunch at the palace? (5 and 6-year-olds)

Joseph's Cup

The brothers woke up in the morning and started on their trip home. They were happy that Simeon was with them.

Just as they were leaving the city, they heard voices shouting, "Stop! Stop! On the orders of Tzafnat Panayach!" They turned around quickly. The chief servant and his men were chasing them.

"What's the matter?" asked Reuben.

"Stop!" yelled the chief servant again. He looked angry.

One of the brothers whispered, "Yesterday he greeted us so nicely in Tzafnat Panayach's house. Today he is angry with us." Then he asked loudly, "Why are you angry? Did we do anything wrong?"

"Yes, you did. You were treated well! We honored you and gave you gifts! And you took Tzafnat Panayach's beautiful silver cup!"

The brothers were shocked. "We don't take things that do not belong to us," said Judah. Don't you remember that we returned the money that we found in our sacks?"

The chief servant said, "My master told me that you took his wine cup. He is the wisest man in all of Egypt and he always tells the truth. The cup must be in one of your sacks."

"All right, look through our sacks," said Reuben. "If the cup is in one of our sacks, you can put one of us in prison." He was sure that the servant was mistaken.

The servants opened the sacks of each brother one by one – Reuben, Simeon, Levi, Judah, Issachar, Zebulon, Dan, Naphtali, Gad, Asher and, last, Benjamin.

"Here is the cup we are looking for!" shouted the servant as he pulled it from Benjamin's sack.

The brothers couldn't believe it. Benjamin especially couldn't believe it. "How did it get there?" they asked each other. Benjamin would never take something that didn't belong to him. Would Benjamin be put in prison? How could they then keep their promise to their father to bring Benjamin back?

"Close up the sacks," ordered the chief servant. "Now we will go back to the city to see Tzafnat Panayach."

Questions on the Story

1. Why did the chief servant yell at Joseph's brothers? Who told him to do that?
2. Why did Joseph want his brothers to come back to the palace?
3. In whose sack was the cup found?
4. What did the brothers think when the cup was found in the sack of grain?

Joseph and His Brothers Reunite

The brothers worried as they were taken back to the city. What would happen to them? At last, they were brought before Joseph.

"Why did you do such a terrible thing? Why did you take my beautiful wine cup?" asked Joseph as the brothers bowed to him. "The one who took the cup must go to prison."

Judah said, "Any of us whom you choose will stay in Egypt except for Benjamin. We promised our father to bring him home and we must keep our promise."

"My order is that the one who stays in Egypt is the one in whose sack the cup was found," said Joseph.

"Oh, no," said Judah. "Please dont be angry with us. When we told our father that you wanted us to bring our youngest brother, he didn't want Benjamin to leave home. He couldn't bear to say good-bye to Benjamin. He still suffers because our brother Joseph is gone."

Joseph listened and then asked, "Why then did your father let Benjamin go to Egypt?"

Judah answered, "We explained to our father what you said — that without Benjamin we could not buy grain and Simeon would have to stay in Egypt. We promised Father that we would take good care of Benjamin. He believed us. We must keep our promise. He still misses his son Joseph."

After hearing this, Joseph could no longer keep the secret about who he was. He ordered his servants to leave the room. The servants left quickly.

Now only Joseph and his brothers were in the room. Joseph stood up. His face was red with excitement. "I am Joseph, your brother," he said suddenly. "I am Joseph whom you sold to a caravan."

The brothers were shocked. They were afraid. They moved back.

Joseph saw their fear. "Don't be afraid. I won't hurt you. Come closer."

They still didn't believe him. They didn't say a word.

"Don't be afraid because you sold me to the caravan," Joseph continued. "It must have been what God wanted. Pharaoh put me in charge of all the food in Egypt so that I could help everyone during the famine. I helped my own family, too – my father, my brothers, and their wives and children. If you hadn't sold me, I wouldn't have come to Egypt. Then no one would have been able to explain Pharaoh's dream. No one would have gathered the grain during the seven good years for the seven bad years. And there would have been no one to give you grain to take home."

The brothers stared at Joseph. They still didn't move. They still didn't say a word. Then Joseph smiled. He hugged each brother. With tears of joy in their eyes, the brothers hugged him, too.

It was starting to get dark. Night was coming. "We're all very tired," said Joseph. "It's been a very important day. Let's all go to sleep. Tomorrow we'll get up early and you will return home. Benjamin and Simeon will go with you. Our father will be very surprised and happy."

Questions on the Story

1. What did Joseph say the punishment was for taking the cup?
2. Why were the brothers afraid when they found out that Tzafnat Panayach was really Joseph? (5 and 6-year-olds)

THEMES IN THE STORY

Joseph's Brothers Come Back to Egypt

When the brothers came to Egypt, a unique situation resulted. Joseph recognized his brothers, but his brothers did not recognize him. To add to this, the brothers could not understand why Joseph accused them of being spies.

Bringing the Theme Closer
- Were the brothers happy or sad to be back in Egypt?
- Why do you think Joseph didn't tell his brothers right away who he was?
- If you were Joseph, would you have done the same thing?
- How do you think Simeon felt when he saw his brothers when they returned to Egypt?

Joseph Reveals His Identity

Joseph behaved in a way that confused his brothers. At first, he honored his brothers as welcome dinner guests in his home, providing them with new clothes and water for their camels. Later, he treated them as thieves. Finally, he revealed himself as their brother.

Bringing the Theme Closer
- Did the brothers like being in Joseph's house?
- Do you remember who put the money back in the sacks? Can you tell what happened then?
- What kind of food did Joseph serve his brothers?
- Would you recognize brothers and/or sisters if you did not see them for a long time?
- Why did Joseph cry when he saw his brothers? Would you have cried in this situation?
- Why do you think the brothers were shocked when Joseph told them who he was? (5 and 6-year-olds)
- Who put Joseph's cup in Benjamin's sack? Why was it put there? (5 and 6-year-olds)

CREATIVE FOLLOW-UP

Retelling the Story

Goals

To focus on the details of the story.
To help the children sequence the events of the story.

ROLE PLAY (3 AND 4-YEAR-OLDS)

Description of Activity

Children communicate with their peers through the use of props.

Materials

variety of sacks
rug piece
large chair decorated to resemble a throne
fancy robe(s)
large decorated ring

Procedure

1. Gather 3 or 4 children together and review the story.
2. Discuss the sequence of events and the personality of each of the characters in the story.
3. Encourage the children to role play specific events and characters for each other in the Bible corner. At circle time the group can role play for the class.
4. Repeat with other groups of children.

ROLE PLAY (5 AND 6-YEAR-OLDS)

Description of Activity

While the teacher narrates the story, children dramatize it using costumes and props.

Materials

robes
scarves
jewelry
ornately decorated large chair
a long table
11 chairs
wine cup

Procedure

1. Ask for volunteers to play the brothers and the chief servant. Performers dress in robes and scarves. The child who plays Joseph dresses in more ornate clothes and sits on the throne. The teacher plays the narrator.
2. Invite those children who are in the audience to dramatize the story for the class.

Building/Creating

MAKE A THRONE (3 TO 6-YEAR-OLDS)

Goal

To help the children understand the role and privileges of a ruler.

Description of Activity

Children make a throne.

Materials

an adult size chair
several strips of colored crepe paper 12" to 18" long
paste or glue
masking tape
sparkles, glitter
piece of carpet (for under the throne)
fabric squares (especially velvet, taffeta, etc.)
scissors

Procedure

1. Discuss the roles and privileges of a ruler (special clothes, special furniture, control over subjects, etc.).
2. Talk about the reasons why rulers sit on thrones. Show and discuss pictures of various thrones. How are the thrones alike? How are they different? Do they look comfortable to sit on? Who would like to sit on a throne? Why?
3. Place a variety of scrap materials on a table, easily accessible to the children.
4. Encourage the children to decorate a particular chair as a throne.
5. Let children take turns sitting on the throne and acting like a king or queen.

Game Time

Goals

To encourage children to take turns.
To emphasize the importance in the story of the hidden wine cup.

WHO TOOK THE WINE CUP? (3 AND 4-YEAR-OLDS)

Description of Activity

Children play a game with a wine cup.

Materials

wine cup

Procedure

1. Children sit in a circle. The teacher chooses one child to sit in the center of the circle with eyes closed.
2. The teacher gives a wine cup to a child in the circle who places it behind his/her back. All the other children in the circle put their hands behind their backs.
3. The child in the center opens his/her eyes and tries to guess who has wine cup.
4. Repeat this procedure until all the children have a turn or the teacher decides that interest has waned.

WHO TOOK THE WINE CUP? (5 AND 6-YEAR-OLDS)

Description of Activity

Children play a game with a wine cup.

Materials

wine cup
song "Joseph You're a Dreamer" from *Bible People Songs* by Jeff Klepper

Procedure

1. Children sit in a circle on the floor, very close together with their hands behind their backs. One child is selected to be "It" and sits in the middle with his/her eyes open.

2. As teacher plays the song "Joseph You're a Dreamer," children pass the wine cup to each other behind their backs. Those who are not passing the wine cup pretend to do so.
3. When the teacher stops the music, "It" tries to guess who has the wine cup.
4. "It" chooses another child to be "It."
5. Repeat this procedure until all the children have a turn or the teacher decides that interest has waned.

Cooking

Goal

To see the connection between the foods we eat today and the foods mentioned in the story.

MAKE SNACK TIME TREATS (3 AND 4-YEAR-OLDS)

Description of Activity

Children taste a variety of foods that are mentioned in the story.

Materials

rice cakes
honey
peanut butter and almond butter (instead of nuts)
napkins
paper plates
plastic knives

Procedure

1. The children set the table for snack time.
2. Place the foods in the materials list on the table.
3. Encourage each child to put one or more of the spreads on a rice cake.
4. Say the proper blessing before eating:

Baruch Atah Adonai Eloheynu Melech HaOlam Shehakol Nihiyeh Bidvaro.
Blessed are you, O Eternal our God, Ruler of the Universe, by whose word all things are made.

This blessing is said before drinking any liquid except wine, or before eating meat, fish, eggs, cheese, etc.

5. Children eat and discuss these foods as they are mentioned in the story.

MAKE HONEY COOKIES (5 AND 6-YEAR-OLDS)

Description of Activity

Children make and eat honey cookies and learn safe cooking habits.

Materials

ingredients and supplies for the recipe below

Procedure

1. Children help to make honey cookies according to the recipe below.

Honey Cookies

Ingredients

> 2 cups flour (minus 1 tablespoon per cup)
> ½ cup sugar
> ½ cup oil
> 1 egg*
> 1 tsp. baking powder
> 1 tsp. honey

*In schools where dietary laws are observed, the following should be done: Break the egg into a glass cup and, with the children, examine the yolk. Discuss what constitutes an acceptable (kosher) egg – one without a blood spot.

Supplies

> 1 cookie sheet
> 1 spatula
> 1 large bowl
> wooden spoon
> 1 small glass cup
> napkins
> measuring spoons
> measuring cups

Method

1. Mix flour with baking powder and set aside.
2. Mix oil with sugar. Add egg, then honey.
3. Slowly add dry ingredients. Mix together. When batter comes away from side of bowl, it is ready.
4. Drop by teaspoonfuls on greased cookie sheet.
5. Bake at 325° for 20 minutes or until golden brown. Cool.
6. Before eating, say the prayer for cookies.

(Recipe from Gittel Schatzow, Rena Rotenberg's grandmother)

TAKING THE STORY HOME

1. Suggest that parents review the story and then encourage their child to use the materials in their Bible Box for dramatic play with siblings and friends. Have them include a large, fancy ring, a robe with decorations, and a piece of fabric to decorate a chair as a throne.
2. Parents and child play *What's in the Bag?* Parents place items such as the following into a sack, making sure that none have sharp points: a wine cup, peanuts, a ring, almonds, and other items unrelated to the story. Use more items with older children. Family members take turns placing a hand into the sack and guessing the identity of the items therein. Older children can also describe the item they feel as other family members guess what each item is.
3. Child and parent make peanut butter. In blender place 1 cup fresh roasted or salted peanuts and 2 to 3 tablespoons vegetable oil. If nuts are unsalted, add salt to taste (about $1/2$ teaspoon per cup).
4. Send home a list of story starters for children to complete. Examples follow:
   - When Joseph's brothers returned to Egypt, they went to his palace where they . . .
   - When Simeon came into the room, his brothers . . .
   - Joseph's brothers brought him a gift because . . .
   - When Joseph saw Benjamin he became very excited. He had to leave the room so that . . .

CHAPTER 14

Jacob, His Sons, and Their Families Go Down to Egypt

BEFORE TELLING THE STORY

1. It is important to establish the continuity of the family of Abraham, Isaac, and Jacob. To aid the children in understanding this concept, review the story of Joseph – how he came to Egypt, his rise to prominence.
2. Remind the children that Abraham also left his country and his home. Refer back to the story of Abraham.

TELLING THE STORY

Joseph Is Alive!

The brothers were very happy when they found out that Tzafnat Panayach was really their brother Joseph. They knew that their father would also be delighted at the news.

Joseph was happy, too. He thought, "It would be good if Father would come to live in Egypt. Oh, I can't wait to see him again!"

Early the next morning Joseph called his brothers together. "Please go back home and tell Father about me," he said. "Tell him that I invite him to live here in Egypt. He should bring all the family – wives, children, grandchildren. He should bring everything that he owns – cattle, goats, sheep."

"But what if Father doesn't want to leave Canaan?" asked one of the brothers.

"Then tell him that the famine will go on for another five years," said Joseph. "There will be no wheat in Canaan. Here in Egypt there is enough wheat for everyone until the famine is over."

"Father will be happy to hear we found you," said Judah. "We'll tell him what you said."

Meanwhile the people of Egypt heard that Joseph had met his brothers. "Did you know that Tzafnat Panayach has an old father in Canaan? Did you know that his other name is Joseph?" they asked each other.

Pharaoh was pleased with the news. He said, "I want Tzafnat Panayach to invite his brothers and his father to come here to Egypt to live. We have enough food to share with them. Tzafnat Panayach saved Egypt from the famine."

Joseph ordered his servants to help his brothers get ready for the trip home. They loaded wagons with sacks of wheat and food and presents. There were presents for everyone in Jacob's family.

Joseph hugged each of his brothers and waved good-bye to them. Then the brothers left. They traveled without stopping. They couldn't wait to tell their father the news.

At last they saw the tents of home. Jacob saw them coming. He ran to meet them.

"We found Joseph," called Benjamin.

"Joseph is alive," shouted Dan.

"Joseph is a very important man in Egypt," yelled Judah.

Then Jacob's sons told him all about Joseph. They told him everything that Joseph had said about the famine. "It's hard for me to believe it," said Jacob, shaking his head.

Jacob looked at the presents which Joseph and Pharaoh had sent to him. He had a big smile on his face. "I must see Joseph again. I will go to Egypt right away."

The brothers were excited to hear this. "Get ready, everyone," they shouted. "We're all going to Egypt as soon as possible!"

Questions on the Story

1. What did Jacob say when he heard the news about Joseph?
2. What would Jacob and his family have to take on their trip to Egypt?
3. What presents do you think Joseph and Pharaoh sent to Jacob?

The Family Goes to Egypt

The wagons and donkeys were loaded with sacks. Everyone was ready to go. Jacob sat in a wagon at the beginning of the long caravan. He was taking all of his family and everything he owned to Egypt. He looked at his sons and their wives and children and animals and at everything that they owned. He felt proud of his family.

The caravan moved slowly throughout the entire day. In the evening they reached Beer-Sheva. They set up camp there. After supper, everyone went to sleep. It had been a hard day of travel. Jacob thought, "We are a very big, happy family. God promised Abraham and Isaac that they would have many children and grandchildren. God kept that promise."

Jacob was happy to be with his big family, but sad to be leaving Canaan. He wondered if he would ever see his home again. Suddenly he heard God's voice. "I know that you are sad to leave your home," said God. "Don't be afraid to go to Egypt. I will take care of you and your family. Your family will become bigger in Egypt."

Jacob felt so much better. He didn't have to worry anymore.

Questions on the Story

1. Why was Jacob sad to leave Canaan? Do you think he will ever go back there again?
2. Why did Jacob feel better after God spoke to him?
3. What do you think Jacob's camp looked like when they stopped for the night on the way to Egypt? (5 and 6-year-olds)

Israel in Egypt

Joseph had prepared places for his father and his brothers and their families to stay. He was excited to see his family again. He and his wife Asnat and their sons Menasseh and Ephraim waited and waited for their arrival.

At last, Jacob arrived in the part of Egypt called Goshen. Joseph went out to meet him. Jacob and Joseph hugged and kissed each other. Jacob stood back and looked at Joseph.

"I haven't seen you in so many years," said Jacob. "I know that you are now a very important man in Egypt."

Joseph had tears of joy in his eyes. "This is a very special moment in my life, Father. I thought I would never see you again."

"Come," said Joseph. "Let me show you where you will live. You and my brothers will all have houses in Goshen. There you will find land for your cattle and sheep."

Pharaoh was happy to hear that Joseph's family had arrived. He invited them to his palace. "I'm so pleased to meet the father and brothers of Tzafnat Panayach. He is a smart and a good person. He has helped the people of Egypt in many ways."

Jacob was proud of Joseph. He and his sons and their families settled in Goshen. They liked it there. They took care of their sheep and their gardens and their children. There was enough wheat for everyone. No one was hungry.

Years passed. Jacob grew older. He called for Joseph to bring Ephraim and Menasseh to him.

"My grandchildren will be like sons to me," said Jacob, and he blessed his grandsons. Then he called all of his children to him. "Reuben, Simeon, Levi, Judah, Zebulon, Issachar, Dan, Gad, Asher, Naphtali, Joseph, and Benjamin," he said, "I am very old. I feel that I will die soon. But first I want to bless each one of you."

Jacob blessed his children. "May each one of you have a large family as I have," he said. "All of your children and grandchildren will be the children of Israel."

And that was what happened. Jacob's children had many children and those children grew up and had many children. The family grew very, very big. They became known as the children of Israel.

Questions on the Story

1. How did Joseph feel to see Jacob again?
2. How did Jacob feel to see Joseph again?
3. Do you think either of them had changed since they last saw each other? In what ways?
4. In the story, when did Menasseh and Ephraim meet their grandfather for the first time? What would it be like for you to meet a grandparent for the first time now?

THEMES IN THE STORY

Jacob Leaves His Country and His Home

Jacob was filled with sorrow to leave the land which was promised to Abraham, his grandfather, and to Isaac, his father. In addition, he was confronted with the conflict of moving to a strange country with a different culture.

Bringing the Theme Closer
- Did Jacob want to leave his country? Why? (Explain that Canaan was the land promised to Abraham by God.)
- How did Jacob feel about leaving his home?
- Did Jacob's sons want to leave Canaan? Why?
- Do you think Jacob will return from Egypt to Canaan?
- Should Jacob have refused to go to Egypt? Why? (5 and 6-year-olds)
- Do you think Jacob will return from Egypt to Canaan? (5 and 6-year-olds)
- This was the second time that Jacob left Canaan for another country (the first was when he ran away from Esau). Compare the two times that Jacob left Canaan in terms of: leaving alone versus leaving with his family, running away versus leaving because of the famine, promising to return versus not being sure about coming back. (5 and 6-year-olds)

Jacob's Family in the Land of Goshen

Jacob and his sons were welcomed by Pharaoh to the land of Goshen. They had a good life there, with homes, gardens, and land for grazing their animals.

Bringing the Theme Closer
- Is it hard to move to a new place? Why?
- How do you make new friends in a new home?
- How do you find things you need in a new city?

Jacob's Blessings

Jacob blessed his grandchildren, Ephraim and Menasseh (Joseph's sons), and then he blessed all of his sons.

Bringing the Theme Closer
- Why was Jacob happy in his new home in Egypt? Do you think he missed his old home?
- Why did Jacob bless his grandsons and his sons?
- Why do parents like to bless their children and grandchildren?
- Have you ever been blessed? By whom? Do you remember how you felt?

CREATIVE FOLLOW-UP

Retelling the Story

Goals
To reinforce information acquired during the telling of the story.
To emphasize certain elements of the story (e.g., caravan, reunion, emigrating).

PAPER BAG HAND PUPPETS (3 AND 4-YEAR-OLDS)

Description of Activity
Children retell the story through hand puppets.

Materials
paper lunch bags
yarn
white glue
buttons
scraps of colored paper
cotton balls
scissors

Procedure
1. Follow the instructions for making paper bag hand puppets on page 92.
2. Gather 3 or 4 children together. Review the story, emphasizing the caravan, the reunion, and emigration to a new country.
3. Teacher and children dramatize different parts of the story for each other.
4. At a later time, the group can reenact the story for the entire class.

PAPER BAG PEOPLE PUPPETS (5 AND 6-YEAR-OLDS)

Description of Activity

Children retell the story through paper bag people puppets.

Materials

large paper grocery bags
paint
white glue
fabric
yarn
cotton balls
scissors

Procedure

1. Follow the instructions for making paper bag people puppets on page 93.
2. Gather 3 to 6 children together. Review and discuss the story.
3. Encourage the children to dramatize the story for each other using the puppets.
4. At a later time, the group can reenact the story for the entire class.

Building/Creating

Goals

To develop an understanding of the different dwellings in which people live.
To help children realize that Jacob and his family lived in a house different from theirs.

COLLAGES (3 AND 4-YEAR-OLDS)

Description of Activity

Children learn about and make collages of various dwelling places.

Materials

My House by Richard Scarry
assorted magazines
scissors

construction paper
glue

Procedure

1. Gather 3 or 4 children together. Show pictures of and discuss the different kinds of houses in which people live – tents, boats, mobile homes, conventional homes, etc.
2. Read the book *My House*, noting the different dwellings shown and discussed in the book. Talk about ways in which these are alike and ways in which they are different.
3. Put out materials in a place that is accessible. Children cut out a variety of dwelling places from magazines and paste them onto construction paper.
4. Discuss what houses were like in ancient Egypt.

CONSTRUCT A SETTLEMENT (5 AND 6-YEAR-OLDS)

Description of Activity

Children build a replica of the settlement in Goshen where Jacob lived with his family.

Materials

pictures of flat roofed houses
large cardboard cartons with tops
small boxes
flat box tops
sand twigs
grass
paper towel rolls
green construction paper
tempera paint in a variety of colors
masking tape
toy animals

Procedure

1. Prior to class make palm trees out of paper towel rolls and construction paper (see above, page 147).
2. Involve children in planning the building of the replica. Decide what to do, how to do it, and where to place the replica in the classroom.

3. Invite parents to participate in the planning and execution of the project. They can also contribute materials and assist in the handling of materials.
4. Let a small group of children work on the project during free play time.
5. Spend several weeks recreating the settlement. Set up the replica on a separate table or on the floor. Include the main characters in the story; the animals, especially cattle and sheep; shepherds, tents, items to place around the settlement (e.g., a well, trees, paths, etc.).
6. Every few days discuss progress on the construction – what has been done so far, what needs to be done.
7. Periodically, send information home with a progress report on the project for parents.

Game Time

I'M LEAVING CANAAN (3 AND 4-YEAR-OLDS)

Goals

To help the children think about necessities for Jacob's trip.
To stimulate imagination.
To help develop, enhance, and enlarge vocabulary.

Description of Activity

Children play a game about Jacob getting ready to leave Canaan.

Materials

Procedure

1. Sit in a circle with the children. Explain to children that they will play a game about Jacob leaving Canaan.
2. Begin by saying, "I'm leaving Canaan and I'm taking something that is . . ." (Describe the item without naming it.)
3. The children try to guess the item that was described.
4. The child who guesses correctly becomes the leader and poses the same question to the others.
5. Continue for 10-15 minutes. Bring the game to a conclusion before children become restless.

I'M LEAVING CANAAN (5 AND 6-YEAR-OLDS)

Goals

To help develop and enhance listening skills.
To help children learn and review the alphabet.

Description of Activity

Children play an alphabet game about Jacob getting ready to leave Canaan.

Materials

set of alphabet cards (one letter on each card)

Procedure

1. Sit in a circle with 6-7 children. (This is a good game to play during free play time.)
2. Explain that they will play a game about Jacob getting ready to leave Canaan.
3. Hold up a card with the letter "a" and say, "I'm leaving Canaan and I'm taking an . . ." (an item that begins with an "a", such as apple)."
4. The next child says, "I'm leaving Canaan and I'm taking an [repeats the item just said] and a . . ." (adds an item starting with a "b").
5. Continue in this manner, with each child repeating all the alphabetical items mentioned previously, and then mentioning another item that begins with the next letter of the alphabet (e.g., apple, bagel, cookie, doughnut, etc.).

TAKING THE STORY HOME

1. Encourage parents to bless their children on Erev Shabbat. Send home a copy of the traditional blessing which parents say:

   To daughters say:

   Y'simaych Elohim K'Sarah, Rifka, Rachel, V'Leah.
   May God make you like Sarah, Rebecca, Rachel, and Leah.

   To sons say:

   Y'simcha Elohim K'Ephraim V'chiMenasheh.
   May God make you like Ephraim and Menasseh.

2. Send home the following instructions for making a sack.

    Materials
    > paper lunch bags
    > scissors
    > paper fasteners
    > felt markers
    > white glue
    > glitter
    > Q-tips

    Procedure
    a. Open a paper lunch bag and stand it up.
    b. Cut off one inch from the top of the bag.
    c. To make a handle, fasten the one inch piece that was cut off to the front right side of the bag and the back left side with paper fasteners.
    d. Encourage the child to decorate the bag. Use felt markers. Then dip the Q-tip into the glue and paint a design onto the bag. Next sprinkle the glitter onto the bag, pouring the excess back into the glitter container. See example below:

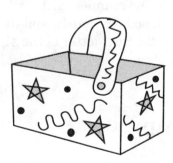

3. Send home a list of story starters for children to complete. Examples follow:
    *   Joseph and his brothers were happy because . . .
    *   Jacob was proud of his big family because . . .
    *   When Joseph and his father saw each other after so many years they . . .
    *   One day, Jacob called his sons and grandchildren together so that . . .
    *   Jacob and his family were happy in Egypt where they had . . .

CHAPTER 15

A Baby Boy in Egypt

BEFORE TELLING THE STORY

1. Review how Jacob and his family came to Egypt. Talk about Jacob and his sons, retracing the events of their lives.
2. Explain that all the rulers of Egypt were called Pharaoh, but that different Pharaohs ruled. The Pharaoh of Joseph's time liked Joseph and the Hebrews. The Pharaoh of Moses' time wanted the Hebrews to be slaves.
3. Refer to the babies discussed in previous stories – Isaac, Jacob, and Esau. Talk about the circumstances of these births and how they differed from those of Moses' birth (e.g., they did not have to be hidden when they were born, their births could be celebrated as Isaac's was, etc.).

TELLING THE STORY

The Slaves

Many, many years ago, all the children of Israel lived in Egypt. They were also known as Hebrews. At that time a new Pharaoh was the ruler of Egypt. He did not like the people of Israel. He was mean to them. He was not the same Pharaoh who had been nice to Joseph and his family. He was a Pharaoh who had never known Joseph. "The children of Israel are too many in number," he said. "I will make them all my slaves."

The children of Israel were forced to build buildings for Pharaoh. They worked every day from early morning until sundown without any rest and without pay. And Pharaoh's guards watched to make sure the slaves kept working, working, working. The slaves were very, very tired when they went home from their jobs. Their lives were very bitter.

Pharaoh was afraid. He said, "I've noticed that the children of Israel have big families. If they keep having so many children they will be a very strong people. Then they might want to fight against me. I have to stop this now! I don't want the boy babies of the Hebrew people to grow to be soldiers. Every time one of their boy babies is born, my soldiers will find him and bring him to me!"

Pharaoh called two women to his palace. They were named Shifra and Puah and they were helpers to women who gave birth to babies.

"Shifra and Puah," said Pharaoh, "when a woman of Israel gives birth, I want you to check to see if it is a boy baby or a girl baby. If it is a boy baby, you must take it away from its parents." But Shifra and Puah knew it was wrong to do that, and they wouldn't help Pharaoh.

The children of Israel were very upset to hear Pharaoh's order. They said to each other, "Oh no! Babies belong with their parents and not with Pharaoh. We will hide the babies after they are born so that Pharaoh's soldiers will not find them."

Yocheved and Amram were slaves. Every day when they came home from work, they said to their children Miriam and Aaron, "We are so tired! The work is so hard!"

One day Yocheved discovered that she was going to have a baby. She and Amram and Miriam and Aaron were so happy with the news! They were worried, though, about what would happen if the baby was a boy. "Don't worry," said Amram, "we'll find a way to hide him."

At last the day came when the baby was born. The family now had a tiny, sweet little boy with sparkling eyes, a small mouth, and red cheeks.

"How will we be able to hide this sweet baby?" they wondered. They kept him as quiet as they could so that no one would know that he was there. Three months passed. The baby had grown bigger.

One day Amram said, "Yocheved, we can't hide the baby anymore. He's too big. How can we keep Pharaoh from finding him?"

Yocheved thought and thought. She walked down to the river where there were tall bulrushes growing. She took a bunch of the bulrushes back to the house. She started doing something with the bulrushes.

"What are you doing?" asked Miriam.

"I'm making a basket for the baby. I'll put the baby in the basket and it will float on the river like a boat," said Yocheved.

Miriam wondered about this. "But how will you be sure that the water won't get into the basket?"

"Let's think about what we can do," said Yocheved. "Maybe we can put tar on the bottom of the basket to keep the water out." And that was what they did.

"Now," said Yocheved, "we'll make a cover to protect the baby from the sun and from insects and birds and so that no one will be able to see what's inside the basket."

At last, they finished preparing the basket. Yocheved wrapped the baby in a blanket and very carefully placed him in the basket. Then she and Miriam went down to the river and placed the basket gently on the water between the tall bulrushes. The water rocked the basket. The baby liked it.

"Miriam," said her mother, "stay here and watch the basket. Make sure that no harm comes to the baby."

Questions on the Story

1. What are bulrushes? (Show the children a variety of grasses, including cattails. Talk about how these grow at the side of a river.)
2. What is a slave? What does he/she do? Why doesn't he/she get paid?
3. What do you think of the plan of Yocheved and Amram for their baby?

The Princess

Miriam did as she was told. She stayed by the river, and watched and watched for a very long time. Suddenly she heard voices. She noticed some girls walking nearby. "What pretty dresses they are wearing," she thought. "I wonder who they are."

Then Miriam saw a beautiful lady wearing the prettiest dress of all. She had a crown on her head. "She must be Pharaoh's daughter, the princess," Miriam thought. "The other girls are probably her helpers."

At that moment, Miriam heard the princess saying, "I see a basket over there. Please bring it to me." One of the helpers picked it up and brought it to the princess. Miriam watched very carefully. No one saw her.

The princess opened the basket. "Look, there's a baby here and he's crying," she said. "This must be a Hebrew baby. He's so sweet, I want to keep him. I'll call him Moses. But I'm not sure that I know how to take care of him."

When Miriam heard that, she jumped out from behind a bush. "I know a woman from the children of Israel who knows how to feed a baby and take care of him," she called. "Shall I get her?"

The princess jumped with surprise. Then she smiled and nodded, "That's a really good idea."

Miriam ran as fast as she could to find her mother. "Mother! Mother!" she shouted. "Pharaoh's daughter found our baby. She wants to keep him, but she needs someone to feed him and take care of him. You can do it. Come quickly!"

Miriam and Yocheved ran to the river. The princess was holding the baby. "Are you the woman to help me with the baby?" asked the princess. "Take him home with you. Take care of him until he's bigger. Then bring him to my father's palace."

"Of course," said Yocheved with a big, happy smile. Then she took Moses home. She fed him and changed him. She kissed and hugged him. She sang songs about the children of Israel to him. When he grew older, Amram told him about the children of Israel and the hard work they had to do.

Moses stayed with his family until he grew bigger. One day Yocheved and Amram said to him, "Next week we will take you to the palace. We are your family, but the palace will be your home. The princess is waiting for you."

The princess was happy to see Moses. "You have taken good care of him," she told Yocheved. Then she said to Moses, "You are a prince now. You will have a servant who will take care of you and you will dress like a prince."

From that day on, Moses lived in the palace and dressed like a prince. But he still thought about his mother and father who had told him about the children of Israel.

Questions on the Story

1. Why did the princess want to keep the baby?
2. Why was the princess willing to let Yocheved care for the baby?
3. How do you think Moses had to act after he became a prince?

THEMES IN THE STORY

The People of Israel Are Pharaoh's Slaves

The idea that a person can be the property of another is unfamiliar and incomprehensible to young children. Through discussion based on key questions, children can be helped to some level of understanding.

Bringing the Theme Closer

*   What is a slave?
*   What is the difference between a slave and a hard worker?
*   How did the slaves in Egypt feel about their lives?
*   How do hard workers feel when they finish their work?

Baby Moses' Family Has a Plan To Protect Him

A difficult task faced Moses' family: to save their son. First, they decided to keep him hidden. When this was no longer possible, they built a basket and placed him in the Nile, watching over and protecting him until he was found by Pharaoh's daughter.

Bringing the Theme Closer

*   What are some of the ways in which Yocheved and Amram could have hidden the baby?
*   How did Miriam feel when she was guarding the basket?
*   Was the princess excited when she found the baby?
*   What did Moses' family think when they learned that the princess planned to take care of Moses?

CREATIVE FOLLOW-UP

Retelling the Story

Goals

To reinforce information acquired during the telling of the story.
To help the children gain greater understanding of the concepts of slavery and freedom.

DISCUSSION (3 AND 4-YEAR-OLDS)

Description of Activity

Children compare life as a slave with life as a prince.

Materials

Procedure

1. Invite the children's comments on how a slave might feel, how a prince might feel; how a slave might dress, how a prince might dress; what a slave does during the day, what a prince does during the day.

DISCUSSION (5 AND 6-YEAR-OLDS)

Description of Activity

Children compare life as a slave with life as a prince.

Materials

newsprint paper
felt marker

Procedure

1. Invite the children's comments on how a slave might feel, how a prince might feel; how a slave might dress, how a prince might dress; what a slave does during the day, what a prince does during the day.
2. As the children contribute information, the teacher writes it on an experience chart to look like the example which follows:

FEELINGS	
Prince	Slave

CLOTHING	
Prince	Slave

DAILY ACTIVITIES	
Prince	Slave

Science

BRICK BUILDING (3 AND 4-YEAR-OLDS)

Goals

To help children understand some science concepts related to this story —
  bricks and their properties, differences between wet clay and cardboard
  blocks.
To help children understand how hard it was for the children of Israel to
  make bricks.

Description of Activity

Children handle and build with blocks and Blockbusters.

Materials

set of Blockbusters
set of wooden unit blocks
wet clay
water

Procedure

1. Children handle and build with a variety of materials, including
    Blockbusters (red brick cardboard blocks), unit blocks, and wet clay
    which they can shape into bricks.
2. Emphasize the differences in the size and shape and texture of the
    materials. Encourage children to experiment with the materials. Discuss
    what keeps real bricks together when building a structure.
3. Talk about how hard it was for the enslaved people of Israel to make
    bricks.

FLOATING AND SINKING (5 AND 6-YEAR-OLDS)

Goals

To help children understand the properties of items that float.

Description of Activity

Children learn about the properties of items that float and/or sink and relate this understanding to Moses' basket.

Materials

large basin filled with water
variety of items to put in the water
felt marker
newsprint paper

Procedure

1. Encourage children to bring to school items which they think might float.
2. Five or six children at a time test the ability of various items to float.
3. Following a discussion of which items float and which sink, the teacher records this information on an experience chart.
4. Talk about the properties of Moses' basket and why it floated.

Dramatic Play

ROLE PLAY (3 AND 4-YEAR-OLDS)

Goal

To help children understand how hard it was for the people of Israel to be slaves.

Description of Activity

Children role play slaves working for Pharaoh.

Materials

pictures of pyramids
brooms
pots and pot scrubbers
dust cloths

fancy clothing
rod

Procedure

1. Children role play slaves. Suggest that one child dress in fancy clothing and sit on a chair. He or she holds a rod and gives orders to the others to "work."

ROLE PLAY (5 AND 6-YEAR-OLDS)

Goal

To help children understand the events of the story.

Description of Activity

Children role play different events in the story.

Materials

pictures of pyramids
brooms
pots and pot scrubbers
dust cloths
fancy clothing
rod

Procedure

1. Review the story.
2. Invite one or more children to role play without talking one part of story (e.g., being slaves, Moses' mother hiding the baby, Miriam watching over her brother, Pharaoh's daughter finding the basket, etc.).
3. Other children guess what event is taking place.

Story Time

READ AND DISCUSS (3 AND 4-YEAR-OLDS)

Goals

To help children begin to understand that traditions and values taught at home are transmitted from generation to generation.

To consider ways that Moses' home life might have influenced his later feelings about slavery.

Description of Activity

Children discuss a book which the teacher reads to them.

Material

The Jewish Home Detectives by Deborah Shayne Syme
My Jewish Home by Andrew Goldstein

Procedure

1. Discuss what Moses' early childhood home might have been like. Encourage the children to offer suggestions.
2. Read *The Jewish Home Detectives* and/or *My Jewish Home* to children.
3. Discuss what makes a home Jewish – symbols, stories, songs, celebrations, the people, etc.
4. Create a Jewish home in a doll house or construct one out of blocks.

READ AND DISCUSS (5 AND 6-YEAR-OLDS)

Goal

To help children understand why something floats.

Description of Activity

Children discuss a book which teacher reads to them.

Materials

Curious George Rides a Bike by H.A. Rey

Procedure

1. Read *Curious George Rides a Bike*.
2. Discuss why the boat in the story floated.
3. Make a boat following the directions in the book.
4. Suggest that children float a boat in the bathtub at home.
5. Discuss what materials were used for Moses' basket that helped it to float.

TAKING THE STORY HOME

1. Suggest that parents take children on a nature walk or visit an arboretum or a botanical garden to look for grasses that might have been used to hide Moses' basket. Notice and discuss the characteristics of the different grasses – length, color, thickness, and shape.

2. Completing mazes helps children develop spatial relationships. Parents encourage child to help Moses get to the palace by tracing his route with a finger or with a crayon, pencil, or felt marker on one or both of the mazes at the end of this chapter. (The simpler maze is for the youngest children.)

3. Send home a list of story starters for children to complete. Examples follow:
   - As Yocheved prepared the basket for her baby, she . . .
   - A long time ago, the ruler of Egypt who was called Pharaoh, . . .
   - Miriam and her mother carried the basket with the baby to . . .
   - When she saw Miriam come running, Yocheved . . .
   - The princess of Egypt came down to the river and . . .
   - While Miriam was watching her baby brother . . .

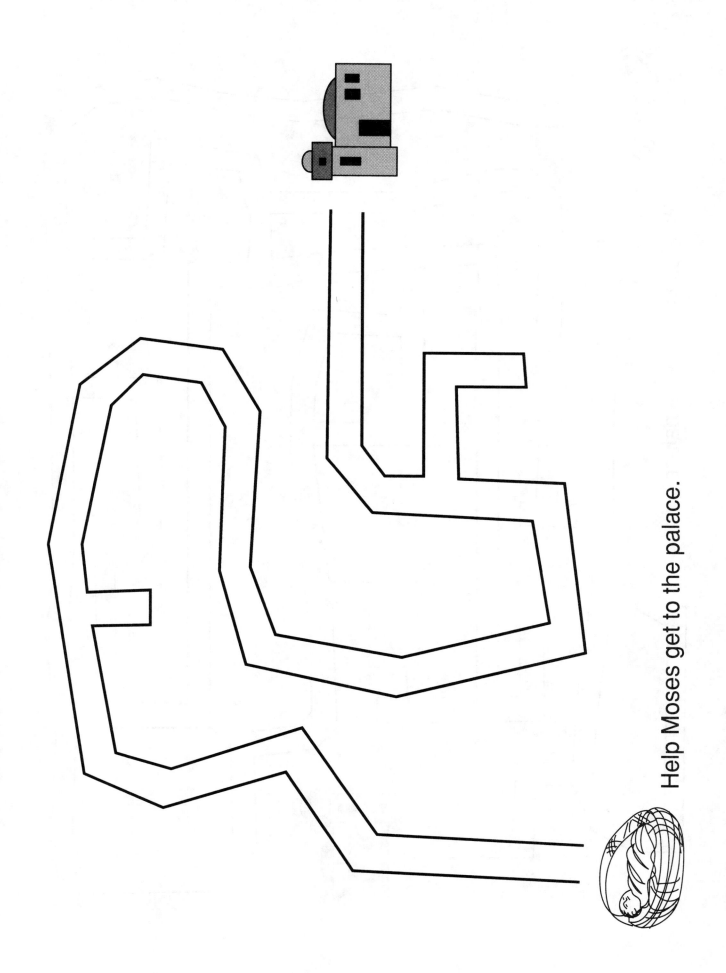

Help Moses get to the palace.

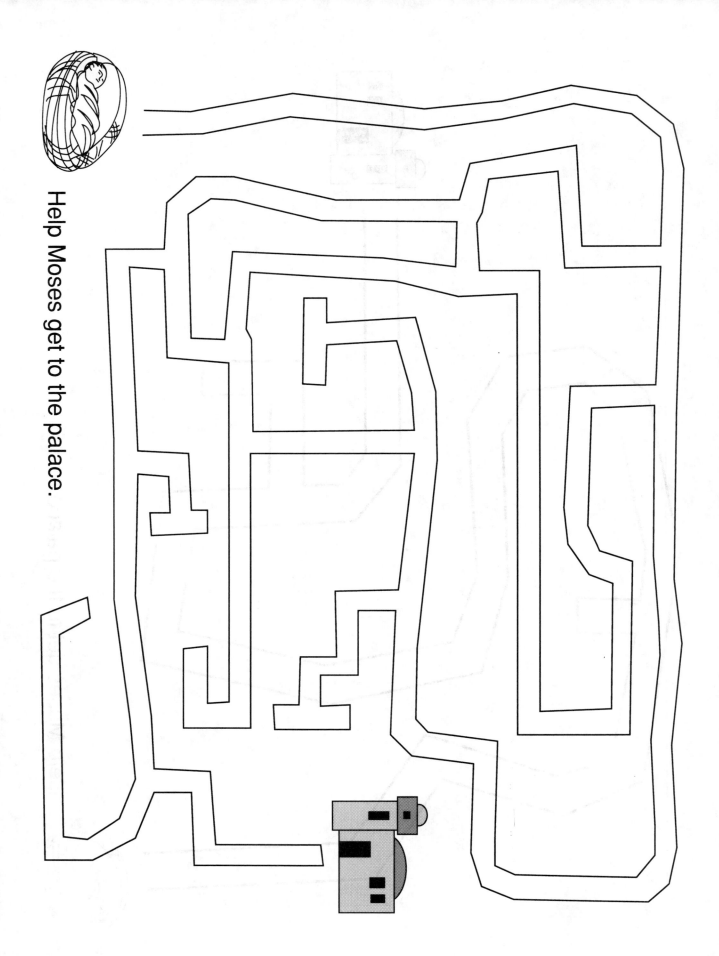

Help Moses get to the palace.

CHAPTER 16

Young Moses

BEFORE TELLING THE STORY

1. Review the life of the Jews in Egypt. Discuss their hardships. Encourage the children to describe the life of a slave.
2. Talk about Moses, his birth and early life, and his relationship with his family.

TELLING THE STORY

Moses and the Slaves

Moses lived in Pharaoh's palace. Pharaoh's daughter was kind to him. She loved him very much. As Moses grew up, everyone in Egypt treated him like a prince. He had a good life.

One hot day, Moses went out walking. As he walked he saw slaves working nearby. One of them was crying, "Don't hit me! Don't beat me!" But an Egyptian guard kept hitting him.

"That guard has no right to do that," Moses thought. "The slave is working hard and the guard is very mean."

"Stop!" shouted Moses, but the guard didn't stop. Moses was very angry. He hit the guard. He hit him so hard that the guard fell to the ground.

"Thank you. Thank you, Prince Moses, for saving me," said the slave. "You've saved my life."

Moses was worried. "Maybe I shouldn't have done that," he thought. He hoped no one had seen what happened, and he didn't tell anyone about it.

The next day he walked to where the slaves were working. He saw two of them fighting. "Stop fighting," he shouted. One of them shouted back, "Are you going to hit me like you hit the Egyptian guard?"

"Oh no!" Moses thought. "Everyone must know about what happened yesterday. When Pharaoh finds out that I hit an Egyptian guard to help a slave, he'll be very angry. He'll punish me. I'd better go away for a while."

Moses walked and walked and walked. He was getting farther and farther from the palace. He was getting farther and farther away from Egypt. He had walked for a very long time.

Moses was tired and thirsty. He sat down to rest near a well. After a few moments, he heard girls' voices, "Let's get some water," they said. "Our sheep are thirsty."

Then he saw seven shepherdesses. They took water from the well and brought it to their sheep to drink.

Moses watched and listened. "Those shepherdesses take good care of their sheep," he thought. "They give water to the sheep even before they take a drink for themselves."

The girls wondered about Moses. "Where is he from?" they asked each other. "He looks like an Egyptian."

Just as the sheep began to drink, some shepherds arrived. They started chasing the girls' sheep away from the water.

"Stop that! Let our sheep drink! They are thirsty," said the girls, but the shepherds did not stop. They wanted to keep the water for their own sheep.

"Leave the girls and their sheep alone!" yelled Moses and he started chasing the shepherds. "You'd better listen to me!" The shepherds were so frightened that they ran away.

"Thank you! Thank you for helping us," said the girls to Moses. When the sheep had finished drinking, the shepherdesses took them home. "We met a stranger who helped us," they told their father Yitro.

"Where is he? Maybe he needs a place to stay. Go back and invite him here," said Yitro.

When the shepherdesses went back to the well, they found Moses sitting there. "Come to our house and be our guest," said Zipporah, one of the sisters. "You were so kind to us!"

"Oh, thank you," said Moses and he followed them home.

When they arrived home, Moses washed his feet and hands and face. Zipporah gave him some food and a place to rest.

Yitro said to him, "You were so kind to my daughters. Please stay with us for as long as you like."

Moses was very pleased. He lived with Yitro's family and became a shepherd. He and Zipporah saw each other every day. They began to love each other. At last, one day they were married. After some time had passed, Zipporah gave birth to a baby boy. They named him Gershon.

Questions on the Story

1. Why did Moses hit the guard? Do you think it was the right thing for him to do?
2. Why did Moses think he should go away for a while?
3. How did Moses help the seven shepherdesses at the well?
4. Was Moses' life with Yitro very different from his life in the palace? Can you think of ways it might have been different? (5 and 6-year-olds)

The Burning Bush

Every day Moses went out to the fields to watch the sheep as they grazed. One day when he was in the field with the sheep, he noticed that everything around him looked more wonderful than ever before. "How beautiful everything is," he thought. "The grass is so green and the sun is so bright." He had a lot of time to think. He thought about Egypt. He thought about the family he had left there and about the Hebrews who were slaves and needed help. "Who is going to help them?" he wondered.

Suddenly he saw a strange sight in the distance. A bush was on fire, but the bush did not seem to burn up. "I must take a closer look at this," he thought.

As he came closer to the bush, he heard a voice calling to him. "Moses, take your shoes off because the ground you are walking on is holy. It's special." Moses took off his sandals.

Then he heard the voice say, "I am the God of the children of Israel. They are slaves in Egypt. I hear their cries. They work so hard. The Egyptian guards are so mean to them. I helped Abraham,

Isaac, and Jacob, and now I am going to help the Hebrew people who are in Egypt. I want you to go back to Egypt and tell Pharaoh to let the children of Israel leave. If he does not do it, he will be sorry."

Moses heard what God said, but he didn't know what to do. "How can I go to the Pharaoh?" he asked. "I am just a shepherd."

"Don't worry, I will be with you," said God.

"But what if the leaders of the Hebrews don't believe that You sent me?" asked Moses.

"I will give you a special sign," answered God. "Throw down the stick that you are holding."

Moses did what God told him to do. The stick became a snake. Moses jumped back. He was afraid. "Hold the snake's tail," said God. As soon as Moses did that, the snake became a stick again.

Then Moses asked again, "How can I speak to Pharaoh? I am a very slow speaker."

"Don't worry," said God. "I chose you to go to Pharaoh even though you are a slow speaker. Your brother Aaron is a good speaker. Take him with you. He will speak for you. I will help you."

Moses left the burning bush and walked home thinking. He told Zipporah all that had happened. "I must do as God says," he said. "Let's get ready to leave." Then they packed clothing, food, and water for the trip back to Egypt.

Before they left Moses said to Yitro, "You have been very good to me. I hope we will see you again soon."

Yitro kissed Zipporah and Gershon good-bye. He was sorry to see them go, but he knew that Moses had to obey God.

Questions on the Story

1. What are some things that Moses thought about while watching the sheep?
2. What did God ask Moses to do to help the children of Israel?
3. What special sign did God give to Moses so that the children of Israel would trust and believe him?

THEMES IN THE STORY

Moses Runs Away from Egypt

Moses was so shocked and outraged when he saw a Hebrew slave being beaten that he could not stand by. He beat the Egyptian taskmaster. Fearing Pharaoh's revenge, he decided to flee Egypt.

Bringing the Theme Closer
- Why do you think Pharaoh would get angry at Moses? What makes you angry?
- What do you think Moses took for his trip? Remember, he had to leave in a hurry.

Moses Meets Yitro's Family

Moses walked through the desert until he reached Midian. There, at a well, he met Yitro's daughters who had come to water their sheep. Moses was a stranger who was welcomed into Yitro's house and family.

Bringing the Theme Closer
- What was it like for Moses to sit near the well and not know anyone? Have you ever been someplace where you didn't know anyone? How did it feel?
- What could Moses do on the long trip so that he would not feel bored? What do you do when you are on a long trip?
- Do you think Moses liked living with Yitro's family? Why? What do you especially like about living in your family?

God Talks to Moses

In previous stories, God spoke to Abraham, Isaac, and Jacob. In this story God speaks to Moses out of a burning bush. He tells Moses to return to Egypt and speak to Pharaoh. God turns Moses' stick into a snake.

Bringing the Theme Closer
- Do you like to be outside on a beautiful day? Do you think Moses liked it?
- Do you think a stick could become a snake? Would you turn a stick into a snake if you could?
- How do you think Moses felt when he was asked to be the leader of the Hebrews? Have you ever been a leader? Did you like being one? Why? (5 and 6-year olds)

CREATIVE FOLLOW-UP

Retelling the Story

PAINTING (3 AND 4-YEAR-OLDS)

Goal

To help children form a concept of the burning bush.

Description of Activity

Children paint their idea of the burning bush.

Materials

bush drawn on drawing paper
several sponges
bowls of red, yellow, and orange paint

Procedure

1. Gather 3 or 4 children together. Review and discuss the burning bush.
2. Provide the materials listed above. Make them easily accessible to the children.
3. Encourage the children to show the burning bush by painting it as they imagine it.
4. At a later time, each child can show and describe his/her picture to the entire class.

I'M GLAD, I'M SAD, I WISH (5 AND 6-YEAR-OLDS)

Goals

To reinforce the important events of the story.
To encourage verbal and artistic expression.

Description of Activity

Children talk about and draw things in the story they are glad about or sad about or things that they wish had happened.

Materials

8 ½" x 11" sheets of newsprint
felt markers

Procedure

1. Before class, write at the top of 6 to 8 sheets of paper "I'm glad." On another 6 to 8 sheets, write "I'm sad," and on still another 6 to 8 sheets, write "I wish."
2. Invite a small group to the table. Each child decides between the sentence starters and picks the appropriate sheet. After drawing a picture with felt markers, the child completes the sentence by dictating to the teacher.
3. Continue with other small groups until everyone has made a picture and completed a statement.
4. Before the whole class, have each child talk about his/her picture and sentence.
5. Display the pictures in the Bible corner.

Story Time

READ AND DISCUSS (3 AND 4-YEAR-OLDS)

Goals

To help children understand differences among people.
To encourage children to help others.

Description of Activity

Children listen to a story and discuss it.

Materials

My Special Friend by Floreva Cohen

Procedure

1. Tell the biblical story, focusing on Moses' speech handicap.
2. Read the book *My Special Friend*.
3. Discuss ways in which people are the same/different (e.g., hair color, color of eyes, height) and ways that handicapped people can help others.
4. Discuss ways that we can help people with handicaps (e.g., helping a child who is in a wheelchair to reach a toy, helping a child who is hearing impaired by standing so that the child can see facial expressions and lips moving, etc.).

MAKE A CHART (5 AND 6-YEAR-OLDS)

Goal

To help children understand similarities and differences among people.

Description of Activity

Children chart similarities and differences among people.

Materials

newsprint
masking tape
felt marker
ruler

Procedure

1. Draw columns on newsprint as follows:

COLOR OF EYES	COLOR OF HAIR
brown	brown
black	black
blue	red
green	blonde
hazel	

2. Following the telling of the story, discuss the colors of classmates' eyes and hair.
3. The teacher fills in on the chart the number of children who have eyes of each color and hair of each color.

Nature Activity

NATURE WALK (3 AND 4-YEAR-OLDS)

Goals

To help children understand the difference between trees and bushes.
To help children understand the importance of caring for the environment.

Description of Activity

Children learn about trees and bushes through observation and discussion.

Materials

pictures of different kinds of trees and bushes found in your area
pictures of trees and bushes found in Israel (good sources are the Jewish National Fund, 42 E. 69th St., New York, NY 10020; Neot Kedumim, P.O. Box 299, Kiryat Ono, Israel 55102; Society for Protection of Nature in Israel, 5 Hashfeyla St., Tel Aviv, Israel)

Procedure

1. Take the class on a nature walk in a park or wooded area.
2. Discuss observations about trees and bushes, noting similarities and differences.
3. Upon returning to the classroom, look at and discuss pictures and posters of trees and bushes.
4. Discuss ways of caring for the trees and bushes (don't tear off branches or bark, be sure they have sufficient water, etc.).
5. Encourage children to draw pictues of the burning bush and of the trees and bushes they learned about.

BLESSINGS FOR FRUITS (5 AND 6-YEAR-OLDS)

Goals

To teach the blessing that is recited before eating various kinds of fruit.

To help children learn the reasons for and meaning of blessings recited before eating.

Description of Activity

Children learn the blessings recited before eating different fruits.

Materials

pictures of familiar fruits that grow on trees (e.g., apples, oranges, etc.)
pictures of trees on which these fruits grow
pictures of familiar fruits that do not grow on trees (e.g, strawberries, various melons, etc.)
pictures of the vines/plants on which these fruits grow
cards on which the following blessings are written in Hebrew block letters.

Baruch Atah Adonai Eloheynu Melech HaOlam Boray Pri HaEtz.
Blessed are You O Eternal our God who creates the fruit of trees.

Baruch Atah Adonai Eloheynu Melech HaOlam Boray Pri HaAdamah.
Blessed are You O Eternal our God who creates the fruit of the earth.

Note: The first blessing is said before eating a fruit which grows on a tree, the second is for a fruit which grows from the ground. (Bananas grow on trees which wither or are cut off and, therefore, are covered by the second blessing.)

Procedure

1. Gather 3 or 4 children together. Show them pictures of different fruits – those that grow on trees and those that do not.
2. Discuss each fruit – where it grows, its special characteristics (e.g., edible skin, peel, pit, seeds, etc.).
3. Review the blessing said for each fruit as the picture is displayed. Ask why and when a blessing is said. Show the cards on which the blessings are written and recite the blessings together.
4. Discuss the correct blessing for fruit juices:

   Baruch Atah Adonai Eloheynu Melech HaOlam Shehakol Nihiyeh Bidvaro.
   Blessed are You O Eternal our God by whose word everything is created.
5. Repeat this with other groups of children until everyone has participated.

TAKING THE STORY HOME

1. Ask parents to talk with their child about how Moses took care of the sheep. The children can then think about how to care for their own animals. If they do not have a pet, suggest they feed the birds, especially in the winter.
2. Send home one or both of the dot-to-dot drawings on the following two pages for children and parents to complete together. (The pyramid is for the younger children and the burning bush is for the older ones.)
3. Send home a list of story starters for children to complete. Examples follow:
   - Moses looked like a prince, and when he saw the slaves . . .
   - Moses left Egypt in a hurry and . . .
   - After Moses walked for a long time, he . . .
   - When Moses saw the bush that was on fire but was not burning up, he . . .
   - Suddenly Moses heard . . .
   - When God told Moses to throw his stick on the ground, Moses . . .

5
10

4

6

9

3

7

2

1 8

Connect the dots and you will see something that has been in Egypt since Pharaoh's time.

Connect the dots to show what Moses saw when God spoke to him.

CHAPTER 17

Moses and Aaron in Egypt

BEFORE TELLING THE STORY

With this story the series of spectacular events leading to the Exodus begins. Review the birth of Moses and his early years, running away from Egypt, meeting and marrying Zipporah, and God's command from the burning bush.

TELLING THE STORY

A Meeting With Pharaoh

Moses, Zipporah, and Gershon walked in the desert for a long time. Aaron was walking to meet them as God had told him. When Moses and Aaron saw each other they were so excited!

"I haven't seen you in such a long time!" said Aaron, as he hugged his brother. Moses said, "I'm so glad you came to meet us. You can help me talk to Pharaoh." When the brothers finished telling each other everything that needed to be told, they continued walking back to Egypt with Zipporah and Gershon.

When they arrived in Egypt, Moses went to visit the Hebrew slaves. He told their leaders of his plan to free them. He knew that was what God wanted him to do. The leaders were thrilled.

"Can you really help us?" they asked. "Don't worry, God will help us," said Moses. "Now Aaron and I need to get ready to see Pharaoh." And they washed their faces, put on clean clothes, and went to meet Pharaoh.

When Moses and Aaron arrived at the palace, a guard at the door said, "You must be Moses and Aaron of the children of Israel. We have heard about you. I will take you to see Pharaoh." Then Moses and Aaron were taken to a big room where Pharaoh sat on a throne. He wore beautiful clothes. His wise men sat around him.

Moses and Aaron stood before Pharaoh. An advisor asked them, "Why do you wish to see Pharaoh?"

"The God of the children of Israel sent us. We are here to tell Pharaoh to let our people go so that they can pray to God in the desert," answered Aaron.

"Who is God?" Pharaoh screamed in anger. "I don't know God. I need slaves. I won't let these people go. From now on I'll make them work even harder. Before, I gave them straw for making bricks. Now they will have to get the straw themselves. Now get out!"

Moses and Aaron left feeling very disappointed. The children of Israel cried when they heard what had happened. "Don't worry, Moses," said God. "Pharaoh will be punished." Moses wondered how it would all take place.

A few days later, Moses and Aaron went to see Pharaoh again. Once again Aaron said, "God wants you to let the Hebrew people leave Egypt."

"And what will God do to me if I do not let them go?" asked Pharaoh.

Moses threw his stick on the ground. The stick became a snake. Pharaoh laughed. "You think that's so great? My wise men can do the same thing. Just watch."

The wise men threw their sticks on the ground. The sticks became snakes. "See?" said Pharaoh. "I told you. Wait, what's happening? Your snake is eating the other snakes." He turned white. Still, he would not let the children of Israel leave Egypt.

Questions on the Story

1. Aaron and Moses had not seen each other for a very long time. What do you think they talked about when they met in the desert?
2. Were the children of Israel glad when Moses came back to Egypt?
3. Do you think God will punish Pharaoh? How?
4. Will Pharaoh let the Hebrew people leave Egypt?

Terrible Things Happen in Egypt

Moses warned Pharaoh that God would punish him if he did not let the children of Israel go. But Pharaoh would not listen.

One day when Pharaoh and the people of Egypt woke up, they noticed that there were frogs jumping everywhere – inside and outside, on their furniture, on their food, and on them! The frogs were all over the place, wherever the Egyptian people lived.

"There's a frog in my oven," said a lady.

"There's a frog jumping on me," screamed a boy.

Pharaoh said, "So what! My wise men can also make the frogs appear any place and any time they wish. They can also make them disappear." Then he called his wise men together, but they could not make frogs disappear.

"Now," said Pharaoh to Moses. "God should make the frogs disappear and I will let the children of Israel go."

The frogs did disappear, but then Pharaoh changed his mind. He did not let the children of Israel go.

One day when they woke up, the people of Egypt saw that it looked very cloudy. Every Egyptian began to itch and scratch.

"There are little gnats everywhere. They bite. It's terrible," the people of Egypt said. There were no gnats where the Hebrews lived.

"There are so many gnats that we can't see the sun," said Pharaoh. "It looks like it's cloudy. Wise men, make the gnats disappear."

The wise men tried and tried, but they couldn't do it. "God made these gnats come to Egypt. We can't get rid of them," they said.

Pharaoh called Moses again and said, "Moses, you and your people can leave Egypt if you will only take away these horrible gnats."

Then God made the gnats go away. But again Pharaoh changed his mind.

When God saw that Pharaoh would not let his people leave Egypt, he punished Pharaoh. He punished him once, he punished him twice, he punished him three times, he punished him four times, he punished him five times, he punished him six times, he punished him seven times, he punished him eight times, he punished him nine times. Each time he was punished, Pharaoh promised to let the Hebrews leave Egypt. But each time after God made the punishment disappear, Pharaoh changed his mind.

Moses warned Pharaoh, "God will punish you once again if you do not let my people leave Egypt. Then you will be very, very sorry."

When God saw that Pharaoh did not let the Hebrews go, more terrible things happened. Pharaoh and the people of Egypt were very upset, but Pharaoh still would not let the Hebrew people leave.

Questions on the Story
1. Why wouldn't Pharaoh let the Hebrew people go?
2. How many times did Moses and Aaron visit Pharaoh?
3. Why didn't Pharaoh want to free the people of Israel?
4. Was it easy for Moses and Aaron to deal with Pharaoh? (5 and 6-year-olds)
5. What did God do to make Pharaoh let the children of Israel leave? Did any of these disasters convince Pharaoh to change his mind? (5 and 6-year-olds)

THEMES IN THE STORY

Slaves in Egypt

The children of Israel were forced by Pharaoh to work under cruel guards and without pay. We are reminded of this bitter and difficult period by some of the symbols found in the Passover Seder (e.g., *maror* reminds us of the bitter lives of the children of Israel in bondage, *charoset* reminds us of the mortar used in building for Pharaoh, and salt water reminds us of the bitter tears shed as slaves for Pharaoh).

Bringing the Theme Closer
- What work did the children of Israel do as slaves in Egypt? (e.g., making bricks from mud, building storehouses with bricks). What kind of work do you do at home? In school?
- What is the difference between being a slave and a hard worker? (e.g., a slave works constantly and a hard worker breaks for meals and rest; a slave is watched by guards, and a hard worker works independently; a slave works without pay and a hard worker gets paid; a slave is forced to work and a hard worker chooses his or her job). What do you get for doing a good job at home or in school?
- Why did the people of Israel feel that their lives were bitter? What does it mean to be bitter?

• At the Seder what reminds us of the bitter lives of the people of Israel? (Discuss the bitter herbs, how they look, taste, feel, smell.) What is your favorite part of the Seder?

Moses and Aaron Visit Pharaoh

The visit to Pharaoh by Moses and Aaron emphasizes the efforts that were made to rescue the people of Israel.

Bringing the Theme Closer
• What did Moses tell Pharaoh? Have you ever been told something important?
• Who wanted to rescue the people of Israel? Why?
• Do you think God cared a lot about the people of Israel? Why? Does God care a lot about us today?
• What do you think of Pharaoh? What was he like? Did people like him? Why?
• Moses and Aaron were simple people and Pharaoh was an important ruler. Who helped Moses and Aaron to deal with Pharaoh? Why? Who helps you when you have a question or a problem? (5 and 6-year-olds)
• What do you think would have happened if God hadn't taken care of the people of Israel? (5 and 6-year-olds)

CREATIVE FOLLOW-UP

Retelling the Story

Goals
To help the children sequence the events of the story.
To help the children interpret the events of the story on their level.

CREATIVE MOVEMENT (3 AND 4-YEAR-OLDS)

Description of Activity
Children dramatize the story through creative movement.

Materials

drum

Procedure

1. Retell the story while beating a drum, changing the intensities of the sound according to the happenings in the story.
2. Encourage the children to dramatize the story through creative movement.

ROLE PLAY (5 AND 6-YEAR-OLDS)

Description of Activity

Children role play with the use of props.

Materials

chair (with fabric to decorate)
robes
crown
stick (for staff)
frogs (made of plastic, paper, or some other material)
gnats (made of black construction paper)

Procedure

1. Gather a few children together.
2. Review the story.
3. Place props in an easily accessible area and discuss them with the children.
4. Encourage the children to assume specific roles.
5. Invite a child to begin narrating the story, involving the others at appropriate places. The following situations may be role played: Moses and his family walking in the desert, Moses meeting Aaron, Moses and Aaron meeting the leaders of the slaves, Moses and Aaron visiting Pharaoh.
6. This group of children can role play for the others at circle time.
7. Other groups of children can repeat this procedure on successive days.
8. Place the props in the Bible corner for use during activity time.

Building/Creating

Goals

To review elements of the story.
To develop fine motor skills.

SPONGE PAINTING (3 AND 4-YEAR-OLDS)

Description of Activity

Children make sponge prints.

Materials

aluminum pie plates
green tempera paint
sponges
newsprint paper

Procedure

1. Cut sponges in the shape of frogs of different sizes.
2. Place the materials on a table easily accessible to a small group of children.
3. Following the discussion of frogs and their relationship to the story, encourage the children to dip the sponges into the paint and make prints on the paper. Display these.

FIGURE DRAWING (5 AND 6-YEAR-OLDS)

Description of Activity

Children discuss the story characters and how each might have looked.

Materials

large pieces of paper
magic markers
white glue
glitter
cotton balls

Procedure

1. Place the paper on the floor.
2. Outline the bodies of the children who are lying on the paper. Each child's right index finger should extend (as if Pharaoh were saying, "No, No, No!" or Moses was saying, "Let my people go!").
3. Each child decides whether he/she will be Moses or Pharaoh and, using the materials provided, decorates the outline as one or the other character.

Story Time

Goal

To show the connection between the Bible story and Passover.

READ AND DISCUSS (3 TO 6-YEAR-OLDS)

Description of Activity

Children listen to a story about Pesach and complete story starters.

Materials

But This Night Is Different by Audrey Friedman Marcus and Raymond A. Zwerin

Procedure

1. Read *But This Night Is Different* to the class.
2. Ask children to complete story starters. Examples follow:

3 and 4-year-olds

- Moses and Aaron did not see each other for a long time. When they met they . . .
- When Pharaoh saw Moses and Aaron, he said . . .
- Moses threw his stick on the ground and . . .

5 and 6-year-olds

- Moses and Aaron made a plan to visit Pharaoh. They decided to . . .
- When Moses stood in front of Pharaoh he felt . . .
- When Moses and Aaron left Pharaoh's palace they said to each other . . .
- Pharaoh would not let the children of Israel go because . . .

TAKING THE STORY HOME

1. Send the biblical story home for parents to read aloud to their child. Parents and child then discuss the following:
   a. What is inappropriate behavior?
   b. Why is it inappropriate?
   c. What is an appropriate response/punishment for that behavior?
2. Send home the dot-to-dot activities on the following two pages (there is one for each age group). Parents and child discuss the picture that is formed and how it relates to the story.
3. The family makes up a poem about Pharaoh (rhyming or not). The parent writes it down and, if the child agrees, it can be brought to school to share with the other children. Send the following home as an example of a family poem on this subject:

   > Pharaoh was a silly man
   > He wouldn't let them go.
   > One day he saw a frog in a pan
   > And then he said, "Oh, no!"

4. Send home a list of story starters for children to complete. Examples follow:
   - To make bricks the slaves had to . . .
   - When Moses and Aaron met in the desert, they . . .
   - When Moses and Aaron arrived in Egypt, they . . .
   - When he heard what Aaron had to say, Pharaoh . . .
   - The frogs in Egypt . . .
   - The punishments of the Egyptians made Pharaoh . . .

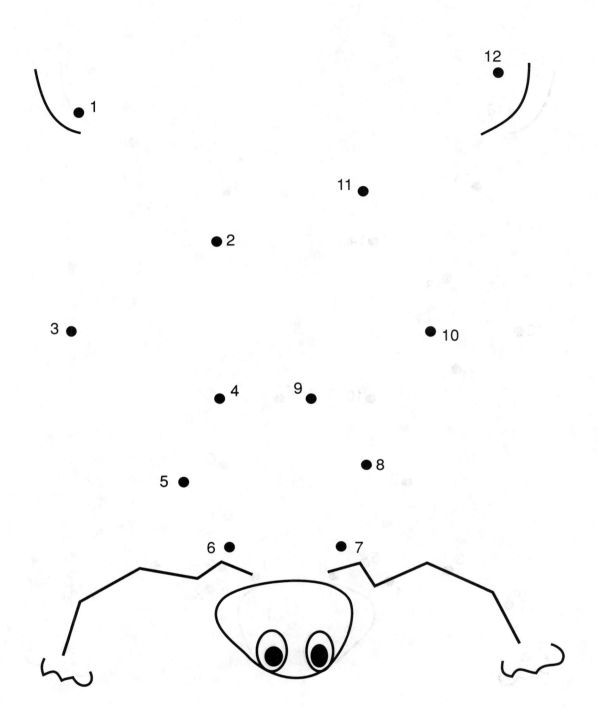

Connect the dots and you will see something that was one of the plagues.

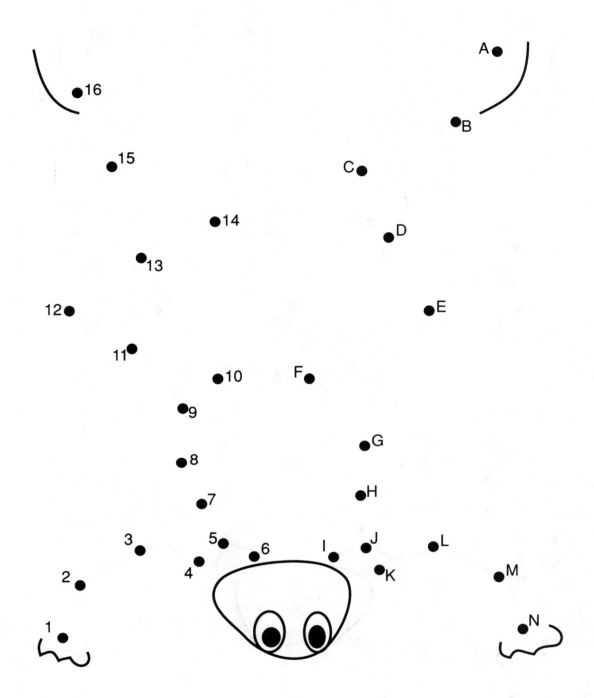

A

B

16

15

C

14

D

13

12

E

11

10

F

9

G

8

H

7

3   5   6   I   J   L

4   K   M

2   N

1

Connect the dots and you will see something
that was one of the plagues.

CHAPTER 18

The People of Israel Leave Egypt

BEFORE TELLING THE STORY

1. This story marks the beginning of the end of the history of the Hebrews in Egypt. It would be good, therefore, to review the following with the children:
   a. How the children of Israel came to Egypt (story of Jacob and Joseph)
   b. The new Pharaoh who did not know about Joseph
   c. The new laws of the new Pharaoh
   d. The life of the Hebrews in Egypt, as slaves
   e. Moses and Aaron going before Pharaoh

TELLING THE STORY

Getting Ready To Leave

One day God said to Moses and Aaron, "Go to the Hebrews and tell them to get ready to leave Egypt."

"Get ready to go?" shouted Moses and Aaron. "Now? Right now?"

"Yes, right now," God said. "I will make something terrible happen to Egypt. This time I am sure that Pharaoh will let all the children of Israel leave. They will be safe. Here's what they should do. They should eat a special meal of roasted meat. They'll be in a big hurry so they won't have time to let their bread dough rise. They'll have to eat *matzah*. They should be all dressed, packed, and ready to go. When Pharaoh tells them to leave, they'll have to leave quickly!"

Moses was excited. He called together all the leaders of the Hebrews. "We have to get ready to leave Egypt quickly," he said. "And there's a lot of work to do. Listen to me and I'll tell you what needs to be done."

The children of Israel prayed to God. They thanked God for helping them leave Egypt. They thanked God for noticing their unhappiness and for caring about them. When they finished praying, they went back to their homes and did just as God had told them to do. Everybody got busy. Fathers, mothers, grandparents, and children all had work to do.

That night, Pharaoh called Moses to the palace. Pharaoh wanted to see him right away.

"Moses, go!" said Pharaoh. "You and all your people must leave Egypt right now. Take all your sheep and cattle. Just go! So many terrible things happened to us last night!"

Moses left the palace as fast as he could. He ran to where the Hebrews lived. "Let's go!" he shouted. "Pharaoh says we must leave Egypt right away! It's midnight. Let's go now, before he changes his mind."

People were shouting to each other. "We're free people now! We're not slaves anymore! We're leaving Egypt and we're going to the land of Israel!" They took their bundles of clothes and food. They took the dough for the bread before it was ready. It hadn't had time to rise. When it was baked it was very flat. They called it *matzah*.

All the children of Israel followed Moses and Aaron. Fathers and mothers carried babies. Little children held the hands of big brothers and sisters. Some grandfathers and grandmothers walked more slowly. Moses and Aaron were the leaders, and God showed them the way to go.

The people said, "Look how God takes care of us. God shows us the way!"

The people walked for a very long time. Suddenly Moses said, "Everyone stop and listen. Something special happened to us. God took us out of Egypt. From now on, every year at this time, all the children of Israel will have a holiday called Passover. We will remember that we were slaves in Egypt. We will remember how God took care of us and took us out of Egypt. We will eat *matzah* on this holiday so that we can remember how we had to leave Egypt in a big hurry. Fathers and mothers will tell their children all about how hard it was to live in Egypt, how God helped the children of Israel, and how Moses led the children of Israel out of Egypt."

All the people listened very carefully. "Yes, yes," they said to each other. "We will have the holiday of Passover every year. We will remember and we will tell our children. Our children will tell their children, and their children will tell their children, forever and ever."

Then the children of Israel continued to walk all day, day after day, and sometimes even at night.

Questions on the Story

1. Why were the children of Israel in such a big rush to leave Egypt?
2. What did the children of Israel have to do to get ready for their journey out of Egypt?
3. What did the bread look like when the dough didn't have time to rise?
4. Why did Moses tell the people to celebrate a holiday called Passover each year?

Pharaoh Changes His Mind

Meanwhile, Pharaoh was sitting in his palace. "What did I do? I need those slaves. Why did I ever let them go? I'm going to chase them and bring them back."

He called his generals, "Get the soldiers ready! Get the horses ready! Get the chariots ready! Bring the slaves back!"

The soldiers did as they were told. Gallop! Gallop! Gallop! The horses and chariots moved very fast. "Onward, faster!" yelled Pharaoh.

The children of Israel walked and walked until they reached the Sea of Reeds. Then they rested. Suddenly they heard the sound of horses.

A man looked over his shoulder. "Moses, Moses," he shouted. "Look who's coming. It's Pharaoh and his soldiers. Help us, help us!"

Moses said, "God helped you before and God will help you again. God will tell me what to do." And he prayed to God for help.

"Hold your stick high above the water, Moses," said God. And Moses did as God told him.

Suddenly the sea was divided and the water formed two walls. The ground in the middle was dry. "Look at what's happening to the sea!" someone shouted. "We can walk on dry land to the other side."

Moses called, "Everyone go across the sea to the other side. Quickly! Hurry!"

Everyone went as quickly as they could go. The sheep said, "Meh, meh," the cows said "Moo, moo," the camel's feet went "kalump, kalump," and the people ran, "swish, swish."

Pharaoh saw what was happening. "Look, all the people are walking on the dry land. Let's hurry so we can catch them."

As soon as all the children of Israel had gone across the sea, Moses raised his stick again and whoosh. From both sides, the water began to come together, to cover the dry land. It was impossible now to walk across the sea.

A little boy shouted, "Look, the water is covering the dry land again. Pharaoh can't cross the sea and catch us." Everyone cried out, "We're free! We're safe now!"

Oh, how happy the people of Israel were. Moses sang a special song. He sang a song of thanks. Moses' sister Miriam was so happy! She loved to dance and to play the tambourine. She called, "All you women, go and get your tambourines. Let's play them together and dance. It's wonderful to be free."

The women danced and danced. The men and boys stood and clapped their hands. All the Hebrew people were thrilled.

Questions on the Story

1. Why did Pharaoh start chasing the children of Israel after he had ordered them to leave Egypt?
2. Why did the Sea of Reeds part? Who made it part? Why did it go back together again?
3. What did the children of Israel do when they were safely on the other side of the sea?

THEMES IN THE STORY

The Preparations for Leaving Egypt

Many Passover observances today are reminders of our enslavement in Egypt and of the preparations for leaving (e.g., baking *matzah* in a hurry, eating *matzah* instead of bread, and roasting meat).

Bringing the Theme Closer
- Encourage the children to relate this information to Passover observance through discussion.
- What do you think they had to do to get ready to leave in a hurry?
- Do you think they could have gone more slowly?
- How long does it take to bake bread? To bake *matzah*?
- In what ways are *matzah* and bread the same? Different? What else do you eat that is like bread or *matzah*?
- When is the special time to eat *matzah*? When do we eat bread?
- Have you ever noticed a roasted bone on the Seder plate? What does it look like, feel like, smell like? Why is it there?
- What do you think the people of Israel said to each other when they heard that they could leave? What do you say when you are about to leave a place?
- Who helped the people of Israel leave Egypt?

Leaving Egypt

Two major elements of the Exodus which are observed in our time are the release of the people of Israel from slavery and the fact that the Exodus occurred in the spring.

Bringing the Theme Closer
- How do you think the people of Israel felt as they left Egypt? Why? How do you feel when you leave school?
- The people of Israel left Egypt many years ago – before any of us was born, and even before our parents and grandparents were born. How do we know about something that happened long, long ago? (5 and 6-year-olds)
- What do you think would have happened if the people of Israel had remained in Egypt? (Discuss the content of the paragraph "*Avadim Hayinu*" from the Haggadah). (5 and 6-year-olds)
- Why do you think we always celebrate Passover in the spring? (Answer: The Exodus occurred in the spring, and we were told to celebrate the holiday at the same time of the year.) (5 and 6-year-olds)

CREATIVE FOLLOW-UP

Retelling the Story

Goals

To reinforce information acquired during the storytelling.
To help the children sequence the events of the story.

EXPERIENCE CHART (3 AND 4-YEAR-OLDS)

Description of Activity

Children communicate their knowledge of the story through an experience chart.

Materials

large sheets of newsprint
felt marker

Procedure

1. Gather a small group of children together.
2. Encourage the children to complete the following sentence: "At the beginning of this story, God told Moses and Aaron. . . "
3. Draw the responses on the experience chart starting at the upper left-hand corner.
4. Encourage the children to supply the subsequent events of the story in the order in which they occurred. Add the information they provide and also a simple drawing to the experience chart. Number each bit of information as shown below:

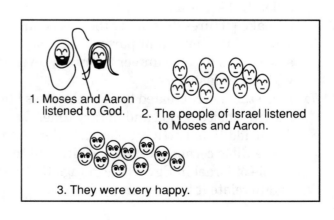

5. As the children tell the events, prompt them with such phrases as "and then what happened?" and "and after that . . . ?"

6. Continue in this manner until the children have finished telling the story.

7. Display the experience chart in an area where the children can see it easily.

8. As an additional activity, place a Seder plate with all the necessary items in the Bible corner. Discuss each item in relation to the story of the people of Israel in Egypt. Encourage the children to identify each item and to relate it to the story.

MAKE A HAGGADAH (5 AND 6-YEAR-OLDS)

Description of Activity

Children think about and sequence the events of the story.

Materials

construction or newsprint paper (approximately 8 ½" x 11")
paper fasteners

Procedure

1. Gather a small group of children together to make a Haggadah.

2. Encourage the children to discuss the events of the story.

3. Provide the materials at easy access and encourage the children to begin drawing any part of the story they remember.

4. Each child describes his/her drawing to the others, telling about the portion of the story to which it relates.

5. After all have described their pictures, place the drawings in sequential order. If there is a major part of the story missing, encourage volunteers to make pictures describing those sections.

6. When all the important parts of the story are illustrated, make them into a book. Ask for a volunteer to draw a cover, then fasten the book together with paper fasteners.

7. Place the newly created book in the class library center for use during the free choice period and library time.

8. As an additional activity, place a Seder plate with all the necessary items in the Bible corner. Discuss each item in relation to the story of the people of Israel in Egypt. Encourage the children to identify each item and to relate it to the story.

Passover Project

Goals

To observe similarities and differences.
To observe the variety in Passover ritual objects.

CREATE A PASSOVER MUSEUM (3 AND 4-YEAR-OLDS)

Description of Activity

Children create a Passover museum with Passover ritual objects.

Materials

Haggadot
matzah covers
Kiddush cups
afikoman holders
small table

Procedure

1. Send a note home asking parents to send Passover ritual objects to school for display. Explain the purpose of the museum.
2. Place all the objects on a table.
3. At circle time encourage each child to bring one object to the circle and describe it to the others.
4. When every child has an object in his/her hands, ask all of those who are holding similar objects to stand.
5. Each child, in turn, returns the objects to the table.
6. Encourage the children to observe the display. Allow them to handle the objects during free play time.

CREATE A PASSOVER MUSEUM (5 AND 6-YEAR-OLDS)

Description of Activity

Children create a museum out of actual ritual objects and those of their own creation.

Materials

Haggadot
matzah covers

Kiddush cups
holders for *afikoman*
small table
tape recorder
tapes of Passover songs
aluminum foil
5 oz. paper cups
man's handkerchief (solid color) or sheeting (solid color) fabric
crayons
scissors
white glue
construction paper
tapestry needle
felt marker
crayons
stapler
hole punch
yarn
5" x 7" cards

Procedure

1. Send a note home asking parents to send Passover ritual objects to school for display. Explain the purpose of the museum.
2. Place all the objects on a table.
3. At circle time encourage each child to bring one object to the circle and describe it to the others.
4. When every child has an object in his/her hands, ask all of those who are holding similar objects to stand.
5. Each child, in turn, returns the objects to the table.
6. Encourage the children to observe the display. Allow them to handle the objects during free play time.
7. Encourage children to replicate out of craft materials any of the objects in the display. Suggestions for making a Kiddush cup, a *matzah* cover, a Haggadah cover, and an *afikoman* holder follow:

To make a Kiddush cup:

a. Cut a piece of aluminum foil to fit around a paper cup. (Foil may be cut in advance by the teacher.)
b. Have each child wrap foil around a cup and press to fit.
c. Insert a plain cup into the first cup and use at the Seder table.

To make a matzah cover:

a. Give each child a man's handkerchief or a piece of sheeting cut to the size of a man's handkerchief and some fabric crayons.
b. Have child draw a design on the fabric.
c. Teacher may fringe the edges.

To make a Haggadah cover:

a. Fold a piece of construction paper in half.
b. Each child draws an appropriate design on the outside fold and, if desired, also writes his/her name there.
c. Laminate the finished product and use it as a cover for a Haggadah.

To make an afikoman holder:

a. Provide each child with two pieces of construction paper. Child decorates both pieces using felt markers and/or crayons.
b. Laminate the pieces of paper.
c. Child or teacher can punch holes around three sides of the pieces of paper.
d. Child or teacher threads a tapestry needle with yarn. Then child sews the two pieces of laminated paper together.

8. After each project is finished, ask the child to dictate a description of his/her object and its use. Write this description on a 5" x 7" card and place it next to the object in the Passover museum.
9. If desired, create a kiosk-like structure for display. Take three cartons or boxes of similar size. Place one on top of the other, with the open part of the middle carton facing out. Mount items for display to the outside of the top and bottom cartons and place them inside the shelf formed by the middle carton (see example below).

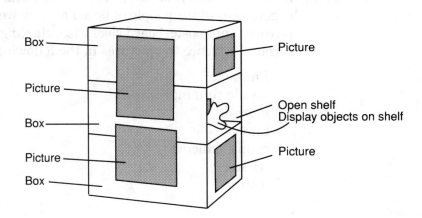

10. As an additional activity, have children record Passover songs on a tape recorder. They may also record Passover sounds (e.g., making *charoset*, saying the Four Questions, pouring water, etc.). Play the tapes at different times for small groups of children. Have them try to identify the sounds/songs.

Game Time

Goal

To help children understand the sequence of events in the story.

LEAVING EGYPT (3 AND 4-YEAR-OLDS)

Description of Activity

Children play a game about leaving Egypt.

Materials

several large pieces of posterboard (preferably white)
felt markers
white glue
scissors
2-6 playing pieces, each of a different color
spinner

Procedure

To make the board:

1. Make the board prior to class. Cut out pictures symbolizing the experiences of the people of Israel as they were leaving Egypt. Glue the pictures onto posterboard clockwise, starting at the lower left-hand corner. Sequence the pictures in the following order:

   Pharaoh
   people running
   matzah
   tambourine
   people dancing
   horses
   a stick

the sea
the sea parted
happy faces

2. Draw connecting squares between the pictures (see example below).

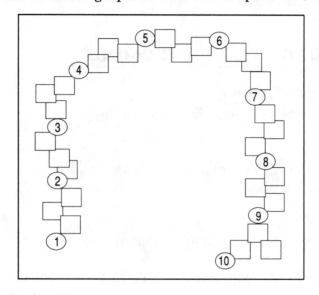

To make the spinner:

1. Prior to class, make the spinner. First, cut out a square piece of posterboard.
2. Draw a line from the top left corner to the bottom right corner and another line from the top right corner to the bottom left corner (see example below).

3. Write the number 1 and 2 alternately in each triangle. Glue dots in each triangle to correspond to the number therein.
4. Attach a spinner to the card at the point where the two diagonal lines intersect.

Directions for playing the game:

1. Each of 2-6 players chooses a playing piece.
2. All players place their playing pieces on the first picture (Pharaoh).

3. Players spin in turn, moving one or two spaces at a time according to the number indicated. If a player lands on a picture, he or she moves to the next space.
4. The first player to reach the last picture (happy faces) waits for the other players to finish.

LEAVING EGYPT (5 AND 6-YEAR-OLDS)

Description of Activity

Children play a game about leaving Egypt.

Materials

several large pieces of posterboard (preferably white)
felt markers
white glue
scissors
2-6 playing pieces, each of a different color
spinner
10 sets of cards with pictures to correspond to the pictures on the board

Procedure

To make the game board and an additional board for each child:
1. Prior to class, follow the directions above and make the board and spinner.
2. Make 10 piles of 8 identical cards, i.e., pictures of Pharaoh in one pile, tambourines in another pile, etc. Write a number in the corner of each card corresponding to the order of that picture on the game board. Laminate the cards.
4. Place the piles of cards in a place that is easily accessible to all the players.
5. Prepare an additional small board for each player. On each square place a picture identical to each of the pictures on the game board and in the same order in which the pictures appear on the game board. An example of a small board follows:

1	2	3	4	5
6	7	8	9	10

Directions for Play:
1. Each of 2-6 players chooses a playing piece.
2. Place the 10 piles of cards in a place that is easily accessible to all the players.
3. Place a small board (see #5 immediately above) in front of each player.
4. All players place their playing pieces on the first picture (Pharaoh).
5. Players spin in turn, moving one to four spaces according to the number indicated on the spinner.
6. As each player lands on or passes a picture on the game board, he/she takes a matching picture card from one of the piles and places it on his/her small board on the picture/number which indicates its sequential order.

Music and Dance

Goal

To encourage the children to interpret the story through creative movement.

CREATIVE MOVEMENT (3 AND 4-YEAR-OLDS)

Description of Activity

Children move creatively while a song about freedom is played.

Materials

"A Song of Freedom" on the cassette tape *Bible People Songs* by Jeff Klepper
scarves
tambourines

Procedure
1. Arrange scarves and tambourines so that they are accessible to the children.
2. As "A Song of Freedom" plays, encourage the children to move freely to the music using the scarves and tambourines.

CREATIVE MOVEMENT (5 AND 6-YEAR-OLDS)

Description of Activity

Children move creatively and sing while a song about freedom is played.

Materials

"A Song of Freedom" on the cassette tape *Bible People Songs* by Jeff Klepper
scarves
tambourines

Procedure

1. As "A Song of Freedom" plays, encourage children to listen to the words and then to act out the events of the story using scarves and tambourines.
2. Children join in singing the chorus each time it is sung.

TAKING THE STORY HOME

1. Have parents show and discuss a Haggadah with their child. Point out the section in which the story of leaving Egypt is told. Family members take turns telling what they know of the story.
2. Invite parents to class in preparation for Passover. After the teacher tells the story, parents and children work together to make the game *Leaving Egypt* for home use. The game can be played by the family as part of the Passover celebration.
3. Send home a list of questions for parents to discuss with their child. Some suggestions follow:

3 to 6-year-olds:

a. What would you have said if you had been let out of Egypt?
b. What are some things we do to remember the Jews who left Egypt?

5 and 6-year-olds:

a. How do we know about the story of Exodus even though it occurred many years ago?
b. Why do you think it is important for us to know and to think about what has happened to the people of Israel in Egypt? (Suggest that parents

stress the fact that those who were in Egypt were our ancestors, and that it is important to remember them and to talk about them.)

4. Send home a list of story starters for children to complete. Examples follow:
   - God told Moses and Aaron to . . .
   - The people of Israel prepared to . . .
   - Moses told the people of Israel to . . .
   - After the people of Israel left Egypt, Pharaoh . . .
   - When he saw Pharaoh's army coming, Moses . . .
   - Miriam was delighted and began to . . .

CHAPTER 19

In the Desert

BEFORE TELLING THE STORY

Help the children to picture the wandering in the desert by providing information about the desert. Talk about the weather in the desert (hot during the day and cold at night), the lack of water, the vegetation (few trees, some bushes and brambles). Use pictures to illustrate some of your descriptions.

TELLING THE STORY

Wandering in the Desert

The children of Israel walked and walked and walked in the desert. There were so many of them! There were old people and young people. There were grown-ups and children. And there were lots and lots of babies. They took all of their things with them – their food, their clothes, and their sheep and goats. They stayed together and kept going. Some rode on donkeys, some rode in wagons, and some walked. They were very tired, but oh so pleased!

They said to each other, "We're so lucky! God has taken us away from Egypt! We are no longer slaves!"

As they walked toward the land of Israel, they got more and more weary and hot and dry. It was a very long trip. Sometimes they wished they could sit under a shady tree and rest with a cool drink. But there are very few trees in the desert and not much water there. Still they kept going. They knew that God was showing them the way to their new home – the land of Israel. But sometimes when they were tired and hot and thirsty, they said to each other, "Maybe we should have stayed in Egypt. Even though we were slaves there, we had water to drink. Even though we worked so hard all day, we had houses to live in. We might starve here in the desert or die from the heat!"

God saw what was happening. He said to Moses, "I will send you bread from the sky. The children of Israel can go out and gather it every morning. They will have enough to feed their families. I will send them more on Friday so that they will have enough for

Shabbat. Then they can rest on Shabbat. I will also send them flocks of birds for meat every day." The people were happy again. "God is taking care of us," they said.

But there was no water to drink. Again the people began complaining. "Maybe we should have stayed in Egypt where there was enough water for everyone. Will we ever get water out here in the desert?"

"What can I do to help the people get water?" Moses asked God. And God told him, "Call all the people together. Then hit a rock with a stick and I will make water come out of it. There will be enough water for everyone."

Moses did just as God had told him. Everything happened just as God had said. Moses and Aaron and the children of Israel were happy again because they had water to drink. Again the people said to each other, "God cares about us! God is taking care of us! Let's keep going until we reach the Land of Israel."

They kept going until their leaders told them to stop. Then they joined together and unpacked their bags and tents. They stayed until their leaders told them to pack up and move again. They hoped that they were getting closer to their new home in the Land of Israel.

Questions on the Story

1. Why were the Hebrew people cranky?
2. How did God take care of the Hebrew people in the desert?
3. Where did the children of Israel plan to make their new home? Who had lived in that place before?
4. Did the people of Israel miss Egypt? Where they disappointed that they weren't going back? How do you know?

The Giving of the Law

One day, the Hebrew people reached a desert called Sinai. They unpacked their bags, set up their tents, and rested at the foot of the mountain. God called to Moses, "Moses, I have taken my people out of Egypt. I took care of them in the desert. Now I want to make them a very special people, like no other people. I want them to teach other people in the world about Me. Listen to Me carefully and then tell the people what I have said. The Hebrews must promise to keep my laws and do as I say if they are to be special."

Then Moses called the children of Israel together. He told them everything that God had said. The people were happy. They shouted, "Yes, yes! We will do as God says. God takes care of us. We will do anything God asks us to do!"

"In three days," Moses told them, "something special will happen. God will tell us what we are to do. We have three days. Now go and wash your clothes and wash yourselves. Let's get ready."

The people were excited! "Quickly, quickly," they said, "we have to be ready!"

One day passed. Two days passed. At last it was the third day. Everyone was ready!

On the morning of the third day, the people heard loud, thundering sounds. They looked up and saw lightning on top of the mountain. There was a dark, heavy cloud there.

"What is happening? It looks so scary," they said to each other.

Moses called to them. "No one shall go up this mountain except me. I will go and bring back the laws. Everyone else stand near the mountain. This is the important day we've waited for!"

Then God gave Moses the Ten Commandments, saying, "I am the Lord your God. Don't have any gods besides Me. Celebrate the Sabbath. Honor your father and mother. Don't murder. Never steal what belongs to others. Tell the truth." God gave the people rules so that they would be able to get along with each other.

Then God said to Moses, "Come up to the mountain. Now I will give you the rest of my laws so that you can bring them down to the children of Israel."

The people stayed near the mountain and waited for Moses to return. They waited for forty days and forty nights. They wondered, "Will Moses come back?"

At last they saw him. He was coming down the mountain carrying stone tablets. His face was shining. At first the people were afraid. "Don't be afraid," he said. "Come and I will teach you God's laws." Then they studied God's laws together.

Questions on the Story

1. What did God want the Hebrews to do in order to become a special people?
2. When Moses heard the thunder on the third day, what did he tell the people?
3. What are some of the laws that God gave to Moses on Mt. Sinai?
4. What did Moses tell the people when he came down from the mountain?
5. How did Moses look when he came down from the mountain?

THEMES IN THE STORY

The People of Israel in the Desert

God helped the people of Israel as they wandered in the desert. Because it was difficult for the former slaves to accept freedom, they complained about the conditions in the desert. In retrospect, Egypt did not seem so bad.

Bringing the Theme Closer
- God helped the people of Israel by sending the manna and the birds. Why do you think God wanted to help them? Have you ever helped someone or some animal?
- How do you feel after you walk for a long time?
- What do you need to take when going on a long walk?
- What did the people think when they received the manna that God sent?

The Giving of the Ten Commandments

Prior to the giving of the Ten Commandments, there was great excitement and anticipation among the people. The laws which were passed down were vital for the establishment and organization of a society. This monumental event, which is central in Judaism, is celebrated and observed on Shavuot.

Bringing the Theme Closer
- What do you think the people said when they heard the rules, the laws?

- What are some rules in your house? In your school?
- Why is it important to have rules and laws?
- Do you know some of the Ten Commandments?
- How do you think the people felt when they heard that God was going to talk to them? (5 and 6-year-olds)
- What did the people think when Moses went up to the top of the mountain? (5 and 6-year-olds)

CREATIVE FOLLOW-UP

Retelling the Story

DESERT COLLAGE (3 AND 4-YEAR-OLDS)

Goals

To help children learn about vegetation in the desert.
To promote the use of fine motor skills.

Description of Activity

Children make a collage of things found in the desert.

Materials

stones
sand
white glue
paste
construction paper
pictures of desert vegetation from *National Geographic, Your Big Backyard, Ranger Rick*, etc.

Procedure

1. Take 3 to 4 children at a time to a table set up with the above materials.
2. Talk with the children about a desert. Explain that it is hot and dry, describe what grows there, etc.
3. Encourage each child to make a collage of things found in the desert.
4. Display the completed collages.

WALL HANGINGS (5 AND 6-YEAR-OLDS)

Goals

To help children understand key concepts of the story through making wall hangings.

To help children learn about vegetation in the desert.

Description of Activity

Children create a wall hanging about the story.

Materials

pieces of felt 2' x 3', one for each child

scraps of felt in different colors

string or yarn

pipe cleaners

scissor

sand

stapler

pictures of things found in the desert – grasses, plants, mountains, shrubs, etc., from *National Geographic*, *Your Big Backyard*, *Ranger Rick*, etc.

white glue

construction paper

Procedure

1. Prior to class, draw an outline of the Ten Commandments on pieces of construction paper.
2. During free play time, take 3 or 4 children to a table which is set up with the above materials.
3. Talk about what it was like to be in the desert, and to receive the Ten Commandments.
4. Encourage each child to make a wall hanging by decorating a large piece of felt. Children may glue sand onto the hanging or paste/staple onto it magazine pictures, yarn, pipe cleaners, and pieces of cutout construction paper and/or felt. If desired, children may also cut out an outline of the Ten Commandments from the construction paper and paste it onto their hanging.
5. Help each child staple a 1' piece of yarn (doubled) to the right and left top of his/her wall hanging.
6. Display the wall hangings in the Bible corner and around the room.

Cooking

MAKE A "MANNA" SNACK (3 AND 4-YEAR-OLDS)

Goal
To encourage children to imagine what manna may have been like.

Description of Activity
Children discuss manna and make a version of it.

Materials
coriander seed
rice cakes
honey
napkins
paper plates
spoons
small paper bowls

Procedure
1. Discuss manna – how it might have looked, smelled, and tasted.
2. Provide the materials listed above. Children combine the coriander seed, rice cakes, and honey as they wish, then taste the "manna."

NAME THE SPICE (5 AND 6-YEAR-OLDS)

Goals
To develop the ability to describe sensations of taste and smell.
To encourage children to imagine what manna may have been like.

Description of Activity
Children taste various spices and herbs.

Materials
a variety of spices and herbs (e.g., coriander seed, dill, oregano, marjoram, basil, bay leaves, cinnamon, etc.)
rice cakes

honey
small paper cups

Procedure

1. In small groups children smell the various spices and herbs. Then they can sprinkle the spices and herbs on the rice cakes and spread them with honey and taste the result. Discuss and describe the various smells and tastes.
2. Children decide whether or not they like their creations and whether or not each tastes as they imagine manna might have tasted.

BAKE MATZAH (3 TO 6-YEAR-OLDS)

Goals

To help children understand the ingredients needed for making *matzah*.
To help children understand the procedure for making *matzah*.

Description of Activity

Children make *matzah* using the same ingredients that were used in ancient times.

Materials

ingredients for recipe below

Procedure

1. Make *matzah* according to the recipe below.
2. After the *matzah* is ready, compare it to other kinds of bread (e.g., rye, white, whole wheat, pita, etc.). Ask the children to describe the differences in taste, touch, and smell.
3. Eat the *matzah* plain or with margarine, honey, or other spread.

Matzah

Ingredients
   1 cup water
   2 cups flour
   $\frac{1}{4}$ teaspoon salt (optional)

Supplies

> measuring cup
> measuring spoon
> mixing bowl
> fork
> rolling pin
> cookie sheet

Method

1. A child puts the flour into the mixing bowl.
2. Another child adds the water to the flour. Add salt if desired.
3. Children take turns mixing these ingredients together with a fork until the ingredients form a doughy consistency.
4. Have each child put some flour on his/her hands. Then divide the dough into pieces about the size of a child's palm.
5. Each child kneads his/her piece of dough for about one minute until the dough is smooth – pressing, squeezing, and squishing it as he/she does with play dough.
6. Have each child make a flat cake out of his/her piece of dough and place it on an ungreased cookie sheet. Prick holes in the cake with a fork.
7. Bake in a very hot oven (450°) for about 10 minutes until brown. Allow to cool.
8. Serve at snack time with any spread (margarine, jam, peanut butter).

Building/Creating

IN THE DESERT (3 AND 4-YEAR-OLDS)

Goal

To help children understand the flora and fauna of the desert.

Description of Activity

Children discuss the desert through the use of visual materials and actual sand.

Materials

pictures and posters of the deserts and its flora and fauna
(good sources of pictures are the Jewish National Fund, the Society for
the Protection of Nature in Israel, *National Geographic*, and National
Wildlife Federation.)
sand
drawing, construction, or oak tag paper
white glue
measuring cups

Procedure

1. Show pictures of sand. Encourage the children to handle the actual sand.
2. Discuss the way sand feels, how a desert might feel, what might and
    might not live in the desert, etc.
3. Discuss how the children of Israel might have felt as they walked in the
    hot sun through the desert looking for something to eat and drink.
5. Prepare a sand table by making designs and wavy lines on drawing,
    construction, or oak tag paper.
6. Children spread the sand over the glue.
7. Let this dry. Then shake off the excess sand.
8. Provide different size measuring cups.

IN THE DESERT (5 AND 6-YEAR-OLDS)

Goals

To help children understand the wildlife and flora and fauna of the desert.
To help children relate to the importance of rules.

Description of Activity

Children relate what they know about the desert for an experience chart.

Materials

pictures and posters of the desert, its wildlife and flora and fauna
(good sources of pictures are the Jewish National Fund, the Society for
the Protection of Nature in Israel, *National Geographic*, and National
Wildlife Federation)
newsprint paper
felt marker

Procedure

1. Show and discuss pictures of the flora and fauna of the desert.
2. Solicit information from the children and write their responses on an experience chart. The following are suggested subjects:
   a. What grows in the desert? What doesn't?
   b. Which animals can live in the desert? Which can't?
   c. Why were rules important for the children of Israel in the desert?
   d. If you were going on a trip to the desert, what would you need to take?
3. Extend this project over several days.
4. If desired, these children may also make a sand painting (see 3 and 4-year-old activity above for instructions).

TAKING THE STORY HOME

1. Have parents talk about manna with their child. Have them emphasize that while we don't know how manna really tasted, we know that it tasted very good and that it reminded the people of honey and spices. The following recipes are sweet and well seasoned and might taste something like manna. Parents and child can make these and enjoy them as treats on Shabbat.

Mandelbrot

Ingredients

3 beaten eggs
6 tbs. light honey
½ cup melted butter
1 tsp. orange rind
1 tsp. vanilla extract
2 ¾ cups flour
2 tsp. baking powder
¼ tsp. salt
1 cup minced almonds
½ cup minced dates
½ cup raisins or currants

Supplies

large bowl
mixing spoon

measuring spoons
measuring cups
baking pan

Method
1. Preheat oven to 375°.
2. Beat together eggs, honey, and butter until light and fluffy. Add orange rind and vanilla extract.
3. Sift together flour, baking powder, and salt. Add to first mixture. Stir in nuts and fruit.
4. Divide the batter in half. Shape two parallel logs, about 2" wide, on a greased tray. Bake 30 minutes at 375°.
5. Slice baked logs into ½" slices. Place slices on the same tray, and return to the same oven for another 15-20 minutes. Remove and cool.

Approximate yield: 2 dozen

© 1972 by Mollie Katzen from *The Enchanted Broccoli Forest.* Published by Ten Speed Press, Berkeley, California. Reprinted with permission.

Honey-Bran Muffins

Ingredients
1 cup unbleached white flour
¼ tsp. salt
1 tsp. baking soda
1 cup raw, unprocessed bran
1 cup buttermilk
1 large egg
⅓ cup light honey (melt together with 3 tbs. butter)
⅓ cup raisins

Supplies
large bowl
mixing spoon
measuring spoons
measuring cups
muffin tin

Method

1. Sift together the flour, salt, and baking soda into a large bowl.
2. Stir in the bran.
3. Make a well in the center. Beat together the liquid ingredients. Pour this into the well in the dry mixture. Add raisins, and stir everything just long enough to perfectly combine. Fill the cups ⅔ full. Bake 25-30 minutes in preheated 350° oven.

Approximate yield: 12 muffins

© 1972 by Mollie Katzen from *The Enchanted Broccoli Forest*. Published by Ten Speed Press, Berkeley, California. Reprinted with permission.

2. Send home a note urging parents to continue adding to and using the Bible Box to reinforce the Bible personalities studied during the year.
3. Send home a list of story starters for children to complete. Examples follow:
   - In the desert, the people of Israel . . .
   - While walking in the desert, the people of Israel . . .
   - At Sinai Moses told the people of Israel . . .
   - God spoke to the people of Israel and . . .
   - When Moses went up to the top of Mt. Sinai, he . . .
   - The people of Israel saw Moses coming down from Mt. Sinai and . . .

BIBLIOGRAPHY

Alda, Arlene. *Matthew and His Dad*. New York: Simon and Schuster, 1983.

> The special relationship between a young boy and his father is described in this book. Includes excellent photographs.

Arnstein, Helene S. *Billy and Our New Baby*. New York: Human Sciences Press, 1973.

> This book helps a child cope with the arrival of a new baby.

Bacigalupi, Marcella, et al. *It's Scary Sometimes*. New York: Human Sciences Press, 1978.

> Sometimes things get scary. When and what is described in this well written book.

Banish, Roslyn. *Let Me Tell You About My Baby*. Berkeley, CA: Harper & Row Junior Books, 1988.

> A young child describes the changes in his household, his family, and himself when a new baby arrives on the scene.

Barrett, John. *No Time for Me*. New York: Human Sciences Press, 1979.

> The very hectic work schedule of a mother and father who are lawyers creates resentment in their child. The resolution of this issue is clearly delineated in this book.

Berger, Terry. *I have Feelings*. New York: Human Sciences Press, 1971.

> This is a wonderful book for young children that expresses and describes emotions.

_____. *Feelings*. New York: Human Sciences Press, 1971.

> A picture book of emotions that is an excellent resource for young children.

Boyd, Selma, and Boyd, Pauline. *The How: Making the Best of a Mistake*. New York: Human Sciences Press, 1981.

> Dealing with the aftermath of a mistake is the theme of this book.

Cohen, Floreva. *My Special Friend*. New York: Board of Jewish Education of
  Greater New York, 1986.

> Written by an early childhood educator, this exceptional book
> describes a unique friendship between two children, one of whom has
> Down's Syndrome.

Cohen, Miriam. *Will I Have a Friend?* New York: Macmillan Publishing Co.,
  1967.

> In clear language this beautifully illustrated book deals with
> relationships among children in a nursery school

Cohen, Mortimer J. *Pathways Through the Bible*. Philadelphia: Jewish
  Publication Society, 1964.

> This is a simplified, readable, version of the Bible.

Cowan, Paul. *A Torah Is Written*. Philadelphia: Jewish Publication Society,
  1986.

> A simplified, picture-full description of the writing of a Torah.

Culi, Rabbi Yaakov. *The Torah Anthology*. Vols. 1-8. Rabbi Aryeh Kaplan,
  trans. Brooklyn: Maznaim Press, 1982.

> Various interesting commentaries accompany this edition of the
> Torah originally compiled in the 18th century by Rabbi Culi (*Yalkut
> Me'am Lo'ez*).

Davis, Moshe, and Levy, Isaac. *Journeys of the Children of Israel*. London:
  Vallentine, Mitchell & Co., Ltd., 1966.

> Maps and information about climate and natural resources make
> this book a good addition to learning and to teaching about the Bible.

Donin, Rabbi Hayyim Halevy. *To Pray As a Jew*. New York: Basic Books,
  1980.

Encyclopaedia Judaica. Jerusalem: Keter Publishing House, 1974.

> Contains detailed information about biblical personalities, critical
> assessment, view in Hellenistic literature,Rabbinic view, Aggadic
> view, view in medieval Jewish thought, modern interpretation, in
> Christian tradition, in Islam, and in the arts.

Fischman, Joyce. *Bible Work & Play Book One*. New York: Union of American Hebrew Congregations, 1966.

Activities for use in the classroom for both older and younger children.

Furfine, Sandy S., and Nowak, Nancy Cohen. *The Jewish Preschool Teachers Handbook*. Denver: Alternatives in Religious Education, Inc., 1981.

Contains chapters on teaching Jewish values, holidays, symbols, and Hebrew, as well as ideas for enriching the classroom environment and involving parents. Good bibliography.

Goldstein, Andrew. *My Very Own Jewish Home*. Rockville, MD: KarBen Copies, 1987.

Things that identify a home as a Jewish home are described and depicted in this book.

Goodis, Karen Lipschutz. *The Learning Center Book of Bible People*. Denver: Alternatives in Religious Education, Inc., 1981.

Suitable for grades 2-4, this book contains complete lesson plans, as well as suggestions for Bible learning centers.

Grishaver, Joel Lurie. *Bible People Book One (Genesis)*. Denver: Alternatives in Religious Education, Inc. 1980.

Suitable for grades 2-4, contains a variety of activities to stimulate Bible discussion. The Leader Guide offers many good teaching suggestions.

_____. *Bible People Book Two (Exodus to Deuteronomy)*. Denver: Alternatives in Religious Education, Inc. 1981.

Suitable for grades 3-5, contains a variety of activities to stimulate Bible discussion. The Leader Guide offers many good teaching suggestions.

Hareuveni, Nogah. *Ecology in the Bible*. Kiryat Ono, Israel: Neot Kedumin, 1982.

Filled with photographs of plants and animals mentioned in the Bible, this book deals with the relationship between the ecology of Israel, the Bible, and the Jewish tradition.

Hazan, Barbara Shook. *If It Weren't for Benjamin (I'd Always Get To Lick the Spoon)*. New York: Human Sciences Press, 1979.

> Sibling rivalry is discussed in an easy to understand manner in this excellent supplementary resource.

Hertz, Dr. J. H., ed. *Pentateuch and Haftarahs*. London: Soncino, 1963.

> This Torah edition, with interesting commentary, is divided into weekly portions and also includes each Haftarah.

Hollender, Betty. *Bible Stories for Little Children, Vol. I*. New York: Union of American Hebrew Congregation, 1986.

> This is a revised edition of a classic in the field. As with the earlier edition, Midrash and Bible text are combined and each is not clearly defined.

Hutchings, Margaret. *Making Old Testament Toys*. New York: Taplinger Publishing Co., 1972.

> This book contains suggestions for making items useful in telling Bible stories – a camel, a goat, Jacob's ladder.

Kargon, Marcia R. *Recipes and Jewish Cooking Experiences for Pre-School Children*. Baltimore: Board of Jewish Education, 1983.

> Chock full of holiday recipes with guidelines for cooking with and by children. This book contains many recipes suitable for use with Bible stories.

Klepper, Cantor Jeff, and Salkin, Rabbi Jeff. *Bible People Songs*. Denver: Alternatives in Religious Education, 1981.

> This cassette contains appropriate songs for learning about biblical personalities. A songbook is also included.

Kolatch, Alfred. *Complete Dictionary of English and Hebrew First Names*. Middle Village, NY: Jonathan David Publishers, 1984.

> An interesting book that includes the derivation and meanings of first names for both boys and girls, as well as the many forms of different names.

Kraft, Stephen. *Workbook for A Child's Introduction to Torah*. West Orange, NJ: Behrman House, Inc. 1972.

> This workbook helps to make the Bible stories more meaningful and relevant through a variety of activities suitable for older children.

Leibowitz, Nehama. *Studies in Bereshit (Genesis)*. Jerusalem: World Zionist Organization, 1974.

_____. *Studies in Shemot (Exodus)*. Jerusalem: World Zionist Organization, 1976. (2 vols)

_____. *Studies in Vayikra (Leviticus)*. Jerusalem: World Zionist Organization, 1980.

_____. *Studies in Bamidbar (Numbers)*. Jerusalem: World Zionist Organization, 1980.

_____. *Studies in Devarim (Deuteronomy)*. Jerusalem: World Zionist Organization, 1980.

> These excellent books, written by a Bible scholar, will provide excellent background in Bible to teachers and parents, as well as expand their knowledge.

Marcus, Audrey Friedman, and Zwerin, Raymond A. *But This Night Is Different*. New York: Union of American Hebrew Congregations, 1981.

> This excellent book compares a regular family dinner with a Passover Seder point by point.

Meilach, Dona Z. *First Book of Bible Heroes*. Hoboken, NJ: KTAV Publishing Co., 1963.

> These stories, while well written and descriptive, mix Midrash with Bible text (especially in the accounts of Abraham).

_____. *Workbook Part I for First Book of Jewish Heroes*. Hoboken, NJ: KTAV Publishing Co., 1963.

> The many activities in this book are particularly suitable for older children.

Newman, Shirley. *A Child's Introduction to Torah*. West Orange, NJ: Behrman House, Inc., 1972.

> This book, which begins with creation, continues with Abraham, and ends with the death of Moses, occasionally mixes Bible text with Midrash without differentiating between the two. The stories are, however, very well written. Many activities and discussions in the Teacher's Guide can be adapted for younger children.

O'Brien, Anne Sibley. *Where's My Truck*. New York: Holt, Rinehart and Winston, 1985.

> This book, suitable for the youngest children, focuses on the issue of putting toys away.

Orlinsky, Harry. *Understanding the Bible Through History*. Hoboken, NJ: KTAV Publishing Co., 1962.

> Written by a renowned Bible scholar, this wonderful resource contains maps, diagrams, and descriptions of archaeological findings.

Plaut, W. Gunther; Bamberger, Bernard; and Hallo, William W. *The Torah: A Modern Commentary*. New York: Union of American Hebrew Congregations, 1981.

> This modern edition of the Torah has very interesting commentaries and comments.

Pritchard, James B., ed. *Harper Atlas of the Bible*. New York: Harper and Row, 1987.

> Clear descriptions and beautiful illustrations and photographs are included in this very detailed book which adds to our understanding and appreciation of the Bible.

Ray, Eric. *The Story of a Torah Scroll*. Los Angeles: Torah Aura Productions, 1986.

> How is a Torah put together? Who writes the words? These questions and more are answered in this book which is filled with photographs and texts.

Rey, H. A. *Curious George Rides a Bike*. New York: Houghton Mifflin, 1957.

> When George, a very young curious monkey, rides a bike, it leads to some interesting adventures.

Samuels, Ruth. B*ible Stories for Jewish Children from Creation to Joshua*. Hoboken, NJ: KTAV Publishing House, 1954.

> In this beautifully illustrated book, Bible text is mixed with Midrash.

Scarry, Richard. *My House*. New York: Golden Press, 1976.

> A variety of houses is described in this very colorful book.

Sendak, Maurice. *Where the Wild Things Are*. New York: Harper & Row, 1970.

> A boy's dream is well told and well illlustrated in this classic children's book.

_____. *In the Night Kitchen*. New York: Harper & Row, 1970.

> The dream of a young child is told in an engaging manner in this beautifully illustrated book.

Simon, Solomon, and Bial, Morrison David. *The Rabbis' Bible, Volume One: Torah*. West Orange, NJ: Behrman House, 1966.

> In this text the commentary is arranged in an interesting manner. Excellent Teachers Guide.

Syme, Deborah Shayne. *The Jewish Home Detectives*. New York: Union of American Hebrew Congregations, 1981.

> What clues can be found to determine that this is a Jewish home? The detective finds out.

Warshawsky, Gale Solotar. *Creative Puppetry for Jewish Kids*. Denver: Alternatives in Religious Education, 1985.

> Wonderful suggestions and complete instructions for making puppets.

Watson, Jane, et al. *Sometimes I'm Afraid*. Racine, WI: Western Publishing
Company, 1971.

> This book clearly describes, from a young child's viewpoint, the
> things that cause him fear.

_____. *Sometimes I Get Angry*. Racine, WI: Western Publishing Company,
1971.

> The occasional anger of young children is depicted in this book.

Weilerstein, Sadie Rose. *Little New Angel*. Philadelphia: Jewish Publication
Society, 1947.

> This collection of stories, some related to holidays, is about a family
> with two sisters and a young baby brother.

_____. *What the Moon Brought*. Philadelphia: Jewish Publication Society,
1942.

> Each of the stories in this book focuses on a family's celebration of a
> Jewish holiday. All of the stories are written in simple and clear
> language.

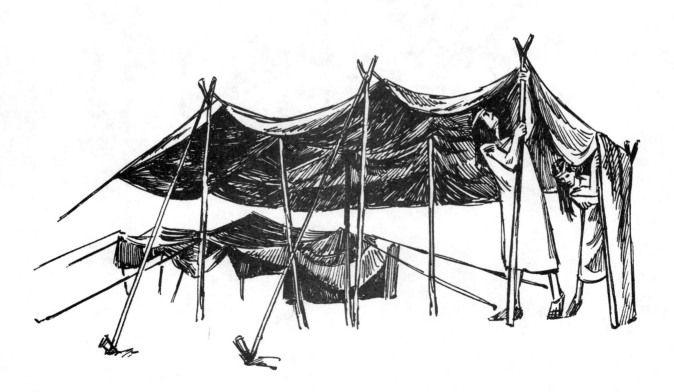

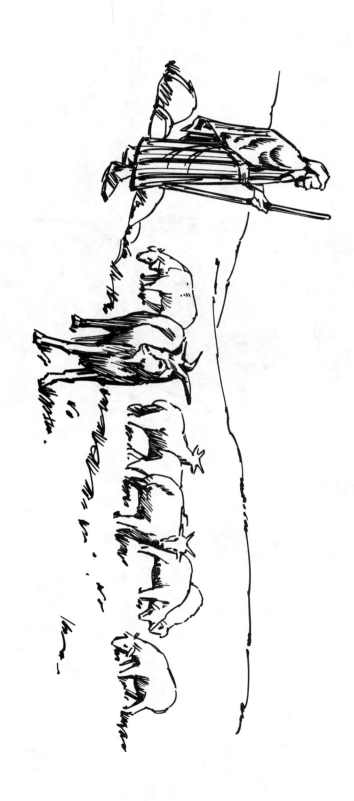

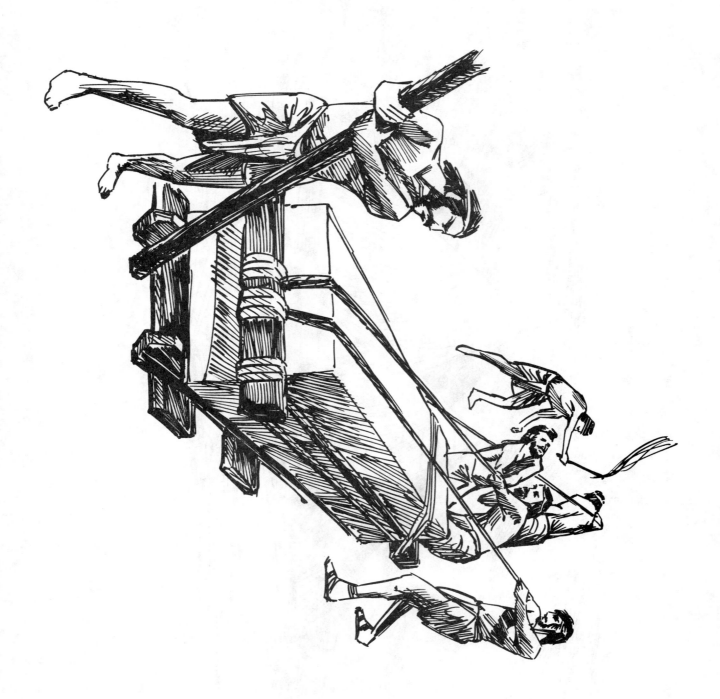

STOREHOUSE